D1428936

Angling

in colour

Angling

in colour

(Sea, Coarse and Game)

edited by
Alan Wrangles

Hamlyn
London New York Sydney Toronto

Published by
The Hamlyn Publishing Group Limited
London   New York   Sydney   Toronto
Hamlyn House, Feltham, Middlesex, England.
© The Hamlyn Publishing Group Limited 1973
ISBN 0 600 30117 6

Chapter Two is taken from 'Fishing Tackle' by Dick Orton
Chapter Six is taken from 'Match Fishing' by Dave Burr and
Jack Winstanley
Chapter Seven is taken from 'Sea Baits' by Jack P. Tupper
Chapters Eight and Nine are taken from 'River Fishing' by
Colin Gamble
Chapters Ten and Eleven are taken from 'Inshore Dinghy
Fishing' by Eddie Wood
Chapter Twelve is taken from 'Competition Sea Angling' by
Bruce McMillen

All the above are Leisure-Plan titles published by
The Hamlyn Publishing Group Limited

Printed by Litografia A. Romero, S.A. Santa Cruz de Tenerife (Spain)

Contents

Introduction

At one time the majority of anglers fished within a relatively small radius of their homes. Their activities were usually quite limited and they tended to specialise in just one of the three types of fishing, coarse, game or sea, and they were content to leave it at that.

The coarse fisherman considered, and often rightly so, that game fishing was beyond his financial reach, and, of course there were thousands who were just not interested in this particular activity.

In general terms most freshwater fishermen viewed sea angling as a pastime dominated by heavy rods, pounds of lead and slippery heaving decks, and for his part the sea angler saw little attraction in catching roach or dace. All sport-fishermen had tended to become rigid in their outlook, and the sport had developed within fairly strict confines.

During the 1950's leisure became more and more a part of everyday life, and as the working week grew steadily shorter and the average man became the owner of transport so he began to look further afield for his leisure activities. He saw almost unlimited possibilities in various aspects of fishing which in the past he had never considered.

The first explosion came from within the ranks of coarse fishermen, their numbers doubled, and then doubled again and within a few years virtually every available stretch of fishing water was taken over, or became controlled by an angling club or association of one kind or another. It is interesting to note the way in which entries to the National Angling Championships leapt forward during this decade. In 1949 there were 77 teams taking part in this event, by 1955 the numbers had grown to 99, and by 1960 there were 101 teams competing. This growth continued throughout the sixties and now this championship is so well attended that it can no longer be held on one venue.

Nowhere in this country is there a site large enough to accommodate the ever growing number- of competitors in the National Angling Championships. This competition is now split into two divisions and is held on two venues.

Sea angling was the next branch of sport fishing to suddenly begin a rapid expansion. Ports such as Littlehampton which during the early 1950's had maybe two or three charter boats operating on a full time basis, suddenly became inundated with anglers searching for good class boats and experienced skippers. Today well equipped fleets of charter boats operate from not only Littlehampton, but also Newhaven, Plymouth and many other ports along the south, east and west coasts of England.

Towns which were completely unknown to the average sea angler twenty years ago are now internationally famous sporting centres. The west coast of Ireland has been opened up by sea angling interests and in the years to come we will hear much about ports in Ulster.

Areas such as the Causeway coast will be visited and re-visited many times by those sportsmen who are looking for the finest of salt water sport.

In the early 1950's few would have believed that eventually gravel pits would be stocked with trout and anglers would be prepared to pay a hundred pounds or more for a season ticket. Even less would they have accepted in those days that a day ticket for trout fishing in some gravel pits would cost £3.50 in 1973. But such is the measure of the popularity of the sport.

As new reservoirs have been built to cater for the ever-increasing demand for water for both domestic and industrial purposes, they have been stocked with trout, so that more and more anglers could sample the delights of this particular form of angling.

Today there is no clear division between the various branches of sportfishing. Coarse anglers, those who love fishing for tench, bream and roach no longer leave the waterside from mid March until mid June. Many of them now take down their fly rods and hunt the wily trout on reservoir and stream. Other coarse anglers go down to the sea during the close season or take holidays in Ireland or Scotland where they indulge their fancy for a change of scene and sport, for a week or a fortnight at a time.

Hardened conger fishers stalk salmon and salmon fishers hunt shark. Such is the modern trend. Today, the sport fishing scene is more alive and colourful than it ever was and in truth it is reflected in this book, 'Angling in Colour'.

ALAN WRANGLES, 1973

Des Brennan

Shark Fishing

While shark fishing is not new in the waters around the British Isles—anglers were fishing for shark at Ballycotton and at Achill back in the 1930's—it is only since the Second World War that this form of sea angling has become really popular. It was not until the 'rubby-dubby' technique of shark fishing was introduced at Looe in Cornwall that anglers began to catch sharks, mainly blue sharks, in numbers and the sport really began to catch on. Garry Culhane who started the angling centre at Kinsale, County Cork, in the late 1950's, introduced the same technique there and in a few short years built a great reputation for Kinsale as a shark fishing station.

Gradually as the technique of shark fishing became more widely known and understood, anglers began experimenting elsewhere and soon 'blues' were being taken in a number of places around the coast. They were found to be more widely distributed than was at first thought and today shark fishing is a feature at many of the better known sea angling centres.

During the season they are plentiful in the English Channel and off the coasts of Devon and Cornwall, but this seems to be as far east in the channel as they penetrate in numbers. They are found up the west coast as far as Pembrokeshire and in Ireland are numerous as far east as County Waterford, which is roughly the same latitude as the Pembrokeshire coast. North of this line they are seldom taken perhaps because the lower temperature and salinity in

(Opposite) Shark fishing is by no means the exclusive province of men, here a successful lady angler displays a blue shark any man would be proud of catching

the Irish Sea does not suit them.

They are found in large numbers off the south coast of Ireland and can be taken along most of this coast. Among the better known places for this type of fishing are Dungarvan, Youghal, Ballycotton, Cobh, Kinsale, Baltimore, and Schull. Though little fished for they are also present on the southwest and west coasts. They are taken at Valentia in County Kerry and in Achill, County Mayo and I have caught blue sharks as far north as Bunbeg in County Donegal. However, they do not seem to range much further north in numbers than the north Mayo coast.

There are few more graceful fish in the sea than the blue shark. It has a long, slim, streamlined body, with long slender pointed and sickle-like pectoral fins. In colour it is a rich steely blue on the back shading to pure white underneath, but unfortunately, the colour fades quickly after death. The razor sharp teeth are triangular in shape with serrated cutting edges, the gill slits are small and the raked-back tail has a long shallow notch in it.

In tropical waters the blue shark grows to a very large size, often 20 feet or more in length, but the fish in our waters are much smaller, averaging around 40 to 60 lb. during the height of the season, and fish of 100 lb. or more are classed as specimens.

Anglers do not fish for them until the middle or end of June when they appear close inshore. They arrive earlier in good summers than in poor ones and their presence coincides with the inshore movement of mackerel, on which they feed. They are more plentiful in fine summers when there is an abundance of mackerel and

13

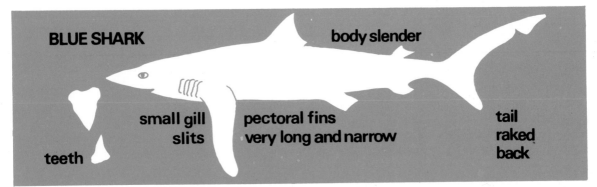

BLUE SHARK

body slender

teeth

small gill
slits

pectoral fins
very long and narrow

tail
raked
back

pilchard on the coast and they remain until the middle or end of September and I have taken good fish as late as the end of October.

They are most plentiful during July and August and during this period smaller fish predominate. But these leave our shores earlier, generally by the end of August and late and early season fish are on average usually larger though not as numerous. The bigger fish are usually females although some big males over 100 lb. in weight are taken each season and the Irish record blue shark weighing 206 lb. was in fact a male. The British record stands at 218 lb. and was taken at Looe, Cornwall, in 1959. Although I once took a baby blue weighing 9 lb. I have not seen a female with young in Irish waters though gravid females have been taken off the south coast of England.

During July and August they are right inshore within a few miles of the coast and I have seen them quartering small bays and coves where there is deep water close in. At this time of year in Ireland at any rate, it is often a mistake to go too far out, but of course a lot depends on the weather conditions prevailing at the time and on the depth of water. They prefer deep water and are seldom found in numbers in depths of less than 15 fathoms. I feel sure that we would enjoy a longer sharkfishing season if we were prepared to go out farther offshore to fish for them at the end of May and in early June as well as in the autumn.

From the angling point of view blue sharks can be very disappointing fish, some fighting exceedingly well, while others put up a very poor show indeed. Part of the trouble lies, I think, in the fact that generally speaking, we fish with gear that is far too heavy and powerful. Most of our fish run on average from 40 to 80 lb. and it does not take heavy rods and 100 lb.

b.s. line to handle fish of this size particularly as they are fish which run far and strongly when hooked. The angler does not have to engage in a trial of strength as when skate fishing. Much lighter tackle gives the angler more sport and a chance to display his skill and gives the fish an opportunity to show what it can do. The longer and harder it runs the quicker it tires itself out. If the fish is caught on very heavy tackle it is usually hauled and bulldozed to the boat and is gaffed before it knows what is happening.

Some of the bigger fish, I am quite sure, do not realise that something serious is wrong when they are hooked. I have seen them literally swim up to the boat on a slack line when first hooked and only come to life when gaffed. They come to life then all right, but by that time it is too late. I have found that fish which come easily to the boat can be frightened by banging on the gunwale or the side of the boat with a hard object. They then take off as if jet-propelled and an exciting time is had before they can be brought alongside again. These fish were not frightened before and this leads me to believe that the actual hooking in the case of some sharks does not upset them as much as one would imagine. Do not get the idea, however, that all blue sharks fight poorly. Far from it, as most of them provide exhilarating sport especially when taken on suitable tackle.

Suitable tackle is no real problem as most boat anglers in these Islands already possess it. All that is required is a light to medium boat rod, a large capacity reel preferably of the multiplier type—size 3/0 or 4/0, and 30 to 40 lb. b.s. line. The reel should have an efficient slipping clutch or star-drag and the handles should not revolve when line is being stripped off the reel. When a shark runs it runs very hard and should the

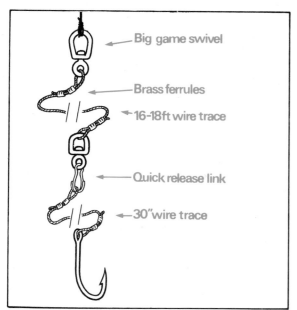

Shark trace

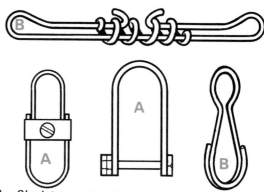

A. Shark trace connectors
B. Quick release attachments

handles of the reel revolve, they cannot be controlled and could be the cause of serious injury to the fingers or hand of the angler. The main line should be of the non-stretch type, preferably a braided synthetic line such as Dacron or Terylene. The only other tackle required is a wire trace, a suitable float, a rod butt-rest, and some spiral leads.

Sharks tend to roll on a trace during the struggle and a long trace is essential otherwise the fish can roll up onto the main line and cut it with its tail or rough skin. A trace of 17 or 18 feet is usually quite adequate though many anglers prefer 20 feet and I have a preference for uncovered cable-laid stainless-steel wire. The plastic-covered wire makes very attractive looking traces when new, but gets very badly chafed after a fish has been played. If the wire is not stainless it rusts quickly under the plastic covering. If the line is joined to the hook and swivels by ferrules which are crimped on, the hold may not be too secure, as the ferrules are crimped onto the plastic covering and are not in direct contact with the wire. Wire of 120 to 150 lb. b.s. is quite suitable and is more flexible and seems to fish better than the heavier gauges.

The trace should bear at least two swivels—the first about three feet from the hook and the other where the main line is joined to the trace. The swivels should be of the big-game type

which are very strong and which do work when under pressure.

The hook link if possible should be joined to the main trace at the first swivel by a heavy spring clip so that it may be readily detached. Sharks have very sharp and dangerous teeth and the extraction of the hook is best left until you are quite sure that the fish is dead. If the hook link is easily detached a new link can be fitted quickly to the rest of the trace and this obviates the necessity of using a whole new trace.

If light tackle is being used it is not advisable to use a very large hook as it can be difficult to drive home on the strike. The hook size depends largely on the size of the bait used, if it is too small it may be blanketed by the bait and the fish may be missed on the strike. A size 10/0 hook is usually big enough for light tackle but a larger hook, say 14/0, is better on heavier tackle. I prefer one with a short shank as sharks can exert great leverage at times on a long-shanked hook and may even straighten or break it. For the same reason anglers often use a heavy-gauge wire for the short hook link as the powerful jaws and teeth of big fish can cut through light wire.

It is very important that hook points should be kept needle sharp and they should be touched up frequently. The knots securing the trace wire to the hook and to the swivels should be securely tied and preferably joined by using rustless ferrules which are crimped on to the wire. Never use a suspect trace. Discard it if you have any doubts about its reliability. Traces are cheap enough if you make up your own and the swivels and hooks can always be salvaged and used again.

Floats come in many shapes and sizes. All one

requires is something which suspends the bait at the desired fishing depth. With a little ingenuity many things can be pressed into service – wine or whisky bottles, plastic washing-up liquid containers, plastic floats, corks, and balloons. There is one serious disadvantage in using bottles or balloons. When the fish dives, water pressure bursts the balloon and a new one must be fitted. When using bottles the line is placed across the mouth of the bottle and the cork is then inserted. This holds the line firmly in position, but when the fish is struck the strain pops the cork out of the bottle and a good supply of bottles is required when the fishing is good.

The advantage of course is that in both cases once the fish is hooked it can be played free of any encumbrance on the line. A float which is fixed to the line should be free to run up and down it. This can easily be managed by putting the main line through the eye of a link swivel and the float can be tied to the other end of the swivel. When the bait is fishing at the desired depth a 'stop' is put on the line above the float to prevent it running further up the line. A rubber band tied to the line or a match-stick secured by two half hitches acts as an efficient stop. The rubber band runs through the rod rings easily, while the match-stick breaks at the top ring.

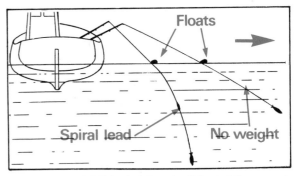

Lead is essential if the bait is to be fished at the correct depth and not washed upwards to the surface by strong currents or fast drift

A few heavy spiral leads – 4 to 6 oz., which can be attached to the line just above the trace help take the bait down to the desired fishing depth. When the boat is drifting fairly quickly the bait does not hang directly below the float, but streams behind it at an angle. Consequently, if say five fathoms of line have been measured off below the float, the bait may not be fishing at this depth. Depending on the speed of the drift it will be fishing considerably nearer the surface – hence the need for some lead to take it deeper. If the boat is drifting quickly a float can often be dispensed with altogether and the bait drift-lined after sufficient line has been paid out to get it down to the required depth.

A rod butt-rest is essential to protect the angler from the butt of the rod, but a rod harness is not necessary unless one if fishing for big porbeagle or mako shark. The last and very necessary part of equipment is a gaff, preferably two. These should be strong with a big gape and should be kept sharp.

The whole secret of blue shark fishing is the use of suitable 'rubby-dubby' to attract the fish to the drifting boat. In the old days at Ballycotton and indeed until quite recently the technique used was to cut up mackerel into small pieces and feed the pieces out over the side, a few at a time. This worked as indeed I know from my own experience, having fished there using this method. However, the use of proper minced or cut up rubby-dubby in a bag which is hung over the side of the boat is far more effective and is now generally accepted. This lays down a nice slick of oil on the surface and a lane of small particles of fish in the water. The use of pilchard, herring, or even commercial cod

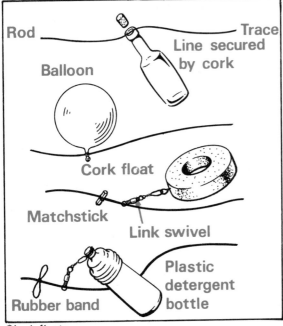

Shark floats

A sharp and strong gaff is an essential item of equipment for all anglers when hunting big sea fish, here it is put to good use to land a fighting shark

liver oil mixed with bran works very well too. The bran soaks up the oil and releases it slowly and if you want to get the oil down deep in the water it is a good idea to mix sand with it. The sand sinks while slowly releasing the oil.

The oily fishes–herring, pilchard, and mackerel, are the best for making rubby-dubby and they are also the best hook baits. Mackerel is the bait normally used as it is the most easily obtained. Whole squid, if available, makes a first class bait for shark. I remember one fine hot week I spent fishing in Kinsale when squid outfished every other bait. It was two days old when I got it and it remained on deck in buckets in the blazing sun all week. Towards the end of the week it was in a terrible condition, smelling to high heaven and it was a real ordeal to put on the hook. However, the sharks would take it in preference to anything else offered to them.

The sense of smell is highly developed among the members of the shark family and many species like the lesser spotted dogfish, depend on it almost entirely to find their food. It is important with blue sharks and this is why rubby-dubby is so successful in attracting them. Rubby-dubby a day or two old and on the 'high' side proves more effective than that which is fresh. It was probably for this reason that the squid outfished the fresh mackerel. Perhaps because of its more powerful odour the sharks found it before they saw the mackerel.

Squid either fresh or slightly off is, however, an excellent bait anyway and sharks can at times be choosey about what they take. Occasionally they will not take a bait unless it is fresh, or may ignore fish like pollack if offered to them as hookbait. Once I hand fed a shoal of four blues with small pieces of mackerel to keep them around the boat whilst we tried to entice them to take whole mackerel offered to them on a hook. They completely ignored the whole fish, swimming past them time after time and it was not until I changed my bait to a small cutlet of mackerel (it looked ridiculously small on the large shark hook) that I induced a fish to take.

For rubby-dubby to be really successful it must be properly used. It should be hung over the side of the boat facing the direction in which the boat is drifting. It should not be suspended in the water, but half in and half out so that as the boat rolls the bag is sloshed about and the oil and pieces of fish are knocked out. A loose mesh

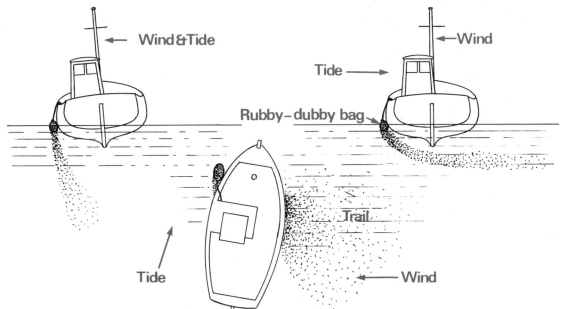

Wind & Tide

Rubby-dubby bag

Tide

Wind

Tide

Trail

Wind

Effect of wind and tide on rubby-dubby trail

bag should be used so that the rubby-dubby can escape. If hung on the other side of the boat sharks may attack it when they swim up the trail, but they seldom swim under the boat to reach it when it is on the other side.

The rate and direction in which the boat drifts is all-important. Fish can only scent what is coming down to them with the tide. They cannot scent what is down-tide of them just as a dog cannot get the scent of anything which is down-wind of it. If wind and tide are running in the same direction the boat drifts quickly, especially if it has a high cabin which catches the wind. If the boat is drifting too fast the rubby-dubby falls beneath the boat or even uptide of it and has little or no effect. If the wind is against the tide it holds the boat back and a nice trail is laid for a considerable distance down-tide. Wind across the tide is even more suitable as a wider area is covered both down and across the tide. If there is no wind at all it makes things very difficult and the only solution is to use the engine slowly to hold the boat against the tide. The same thing can be done when wind and tide are running in the same direction.

Sharking is very much a waiting game and long periods can elapse without meeting a fish. At times inexperienced anglers may get disheartened or tire of the lack of action and decide to move elsewhere and try another drift. This is a mistake. The sharks may be anywhere and one can at any time come across your rubby-

dubby trail and swim up to investigate its source. To shift grounds is to break the trail you may have spent hours laying down and all your efforts are then wasted. For the same reason it is important not to break the continuity of the trail when the rubby-dubby bag is almost empty and in need of renewing. Do not take it out of the water to refill it as any shark swimming up the trail comes to a dead end at the break in the trail and will be unable to find the boat.

Always have two bags—one in the water and the other ready to put over the side *before* the other is taken on board for a refill. I have found that it pays to persevere with a trail once started and that it is also important to keep a watchful eye on the condition of the rubby-dubby bag. The oil and small pieces of fish are washed out of the bag quite quickly and unless changed frequently an effective trail will not be laid.

Rubby-dubby can also be used when fishing to an anchor if there is a good run of tide, although I have not found this method anything like as successful as drifting and have only taken a small number of fish this way. When bottom fishing to an anchor it is a good idea to leave one shark rod fishing, but care must be taken that the line does not foul the lines of other anglers when the tide becomes slack or changes direction. Frequently when bottom fishing, anglers find that fish which they have hooked and are playing are chopped in two by sharks. If a large bait is lowered down on a shark trace it is almost certain to be taken. On occasion sharks can take up station beneath a boat knocking off fish after fish as the angler reels in. This can be very annoying if one is not interested in sharks and the only solution is either to catch the sharks or shift to other grounds.

Normally three, or at the most four, rods are as many as can be effectively fished from one boat without the lines fouling each other, though of choice I would not fish more than three. The rods should be spaced as far apart as possible and the floats fished at different distances from the boat to enable them to stay clear of each other. It is a good idea when starting to fish to have the baits at different depths, i.e. a few fathoms below the surface, in mid-water, and a few fathoms off the bottom, until the fish are found. Then all three anglers can fish at the one depth.

Blue sharks are a pelagic species feeding mainly on shoal fishes such as herring, mackerel, or pilchard, and the bulk of them are taken in the top five fathoms. However, they are often found feeding on shoals of whiting and then they may well be swimming deep, near the bottom. Indeed when the mackerel are scarce or scattered by bad weather, blue sharks often feed on demersal species of fish and are to be found right on the bottom.

The bait and trace should be lowered over the side and sufficient line measured off so that it

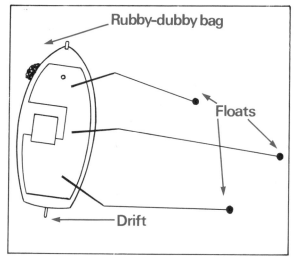

Rubby-dubby bag

Floats

Drift

Spacing of floats when shark fishing to prevent the baits from fishing too close to one another

fishes at the correct depth and then the 'stop' placed on the line. The float can then be allowed to move from the boat for 20 or 30 yards. There is no need to fish it very far from the boat. The reel should be put on check and in free spool. If the check is not strong enough to hold the line on the reel then the reel should be engaged and the tension on the star drag adjusted so that it barely holds, but ensures that when the shark takes it can strip the line freely from the reel. There is nothing further to do then but to sit back and wait.

Shark fishing is a lazy, relaxed form of fishing, interrupted by hectic bouts of action. A fish may come to the boat within minutes of starting to fish or it may be hours before anyone gets a run. Sometimes a shark's fin may be seen cutting through the water as it swims up the rubby-dubby trail then disappears as it sights the bait and dives for it.

At other times the first indication of a shark's presence is an electrifying screech from the reel as the fish runs with the bait, stripping line at a rate of knots. Normally a whole fish is used as bait and the shark must be given time to get a proper hold. When using large baits the shark should be struck as soon as it starts its second run. At times it is not easy to know when, for the first run may be very short and merge into the second. When in doubt—strike, for if the fish is given too long it may either drop the bait or swallow it and become hooked in the stomach. Neither result is desirable. If given too long it may also take more than one bait and the inevitable mess of tangled lines and traces has to be seen to be believed.

Immediately a fish is hooked the other rods should be taken in. Not for the sake of courtesy alone, but to avoid the danger of the fish fouling the other lines and making a hopeless tangle. If the shark is finicky and messes about with the bait without taking it, as they sometimes do, it is a good idea to reel the bait in slowly. This frequently goads the fish into taking a bait it might otherwise drop.

Sharks should be fully played out before they are brought to the gaff. A green fish still full of fight and vigour is dangerous in any boat as it thrashes madly about looking for something into which it can sink its teeth. If tackle is left lying carelessly around its lashing tail can create havoc, so before a fish comes aboard make sure

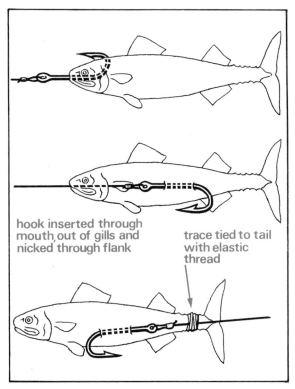

hook inserted through mouth out of gills and nicked through flank

trace tied to tail with elastic thread

Various methods of mounting a shark bait

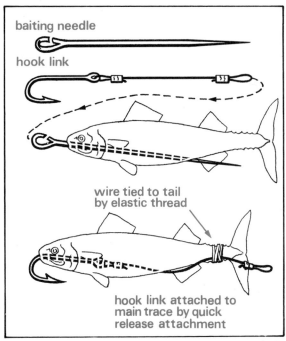

baiting needle

hook link

wire tied to tail by elastic thread

hook link attached to main trace by quick release attachment

The use of the baiting needle when mounting whole fish

that the decks are clear and that all rods are safely stowed out of the way. The fish should be gaffed first near the vent and the tail lifted out of the water. The second gaff should be inserted near the head and the fish lifted into the boat. It can quickly be quietened by a few heavy blows on the snout with a hard heavy object.

One aspect with which I have not yet dealt, is how to bait up. The usual bait is a whole mackerel and there are a number of ways in which it can be mounted. The mackerel can be hooked quite simply through the tail or through the mouth. The hook can be inserted through the mouth, out of the gills and hooked lightly about half way along the side so that the hook and shank lie flat against the body. The bait can also be hooked through the stomach about half way along and the shank and wire laid flat against the body and the wire secured to the tail by some light line or elastic thread. The hook can be buried in the fish by inserting a baiting needle through the vent and out of the mouth. The short hook link is then hooked into the end of the needle and the trace wire is drawn through and out of the bait until the shank is inside the fish and only the hook point protrudes from the mouth. The mackerel can also be slit along the back, the hook inserted so that only the point projects and then the fish is sewn up again with some light line. The last two methods make a very neat job of the bait.

There are many schools of thought on which is the best method, but I have tried them all and cannot really say which is the best, for they have all proved effective. The only provision I would make is that the bait should lie straight and not bunch up on the hook. It should be securely tied, if necessary, to prevent this happening.

Shark fishing sounds and in fact is easy, provided the angler knows what he is doing and avoids certain elementary mistakes. Perhaps the beginner will have a clearer picture in his mind if I describe a typical day's fishing for blue shark.

A fresh south-westerly force 4–5 wind was blowing as John Casey, Alfie Nicholson and I set out from Dungarvan, County Waterford, in Alfie's boat early one July morning. The tide was due to start ebbing in about an hour and we expected to have a good day, for the wind would hold our boat nicely against the tide and edge us partly across it. We stopped just inside Helvic Head at the mouth of Dungarvan Bay to feather

for mackerel. We were lucky, for shoals of mackerel were concentrated here feeding on sprat and with three rods working a string of feathers each the deck was soon covered with their glistening, vibrating bodies.

We would need a lot of mackerel for the rubby-dubby. Normally this would have been prepared a day or two in advance but we had only decided late the previous evening to go fishing. As soon as we had enough mackerel Alfie headed the boat due south and John and I got down to the task of making up the rubby-dubby. This is not an enviable job, particularly in a rough sea and not one to be recommended to those with weak stomachs or a tendency to suffer from sea sickness. On well run professional boats catering for shark fishing the rubby-dubby is seldom seen by anglers, having been prepared beforehand and kept in tightly sealed plastic buckets so that the unpleasant odour does not upset the clients.

We cut up the mackerel into small pieces on a wooden board specially brought for the task and when the bucket was full, pounded the mackerel

Potentially one of the most dangerous moments in angling, a writhing, thrashing, and very angry shark is hauled aboard

into mush with the aid of a heavy baulk of timber. A mincer does a better job of making rubby-dubby, but it needs to be a large one for the fins, gills and skin of the mackerel clog the openings in a small mincer. We filled two old sacks with the rubby-dubby having first added some fish oil and then filled the bucket once again. Satisfied that we had enough we washed down the deck so that it would not become slippery and then set about assembling the three rods and reels and attaching floats and traces.

By the time we were finished we were about three miles off Helvic Head and soon Alfie stopped the engines and allowed the boat to drift. We were in deep water, 25 to 30 fathoms and our drift would take us westwards towards Mine Head. (I find that one must be in deep water—15 fathoms or more, to catch blue sharks in numbers. They do come very close inshore provided there is sufficient depth but in shallow water, although I have taken the

occasional fish, they have all been small.)

As soon as the boat settled down on the drift we put one bag of rubby-dubby over the side after making a number of small holes and cuts in the bag with a knife. When we were satisfied that it was working properly and a nice stream of oil and small pieces of fish was going under the boat and away downtide, we mounted fresh mackerel on the hooks and put them over the side. We had decided to fish near the surface, so after measuring off five or six fathoms of line above the trace we fixed match-sticks to the line above the floats with two half hitches, paid out the line and let the baits and floats drift away from the boat. (There is no need to fish a long way from the boat, 15 to 30 yards is sufficient, but the floats should be kept well separated from each other to avoid a tangle and also to prevent the danger of a shark taking two baits together.)

The reels were then put on check and I had to put mine in gear and adjust the slipping clutch until it barely held the line as my check was too weak to do so on its own. It is important that when a shark takes, it feels the minimum of resistance and can strip line freely off the reel. It was still quite early so we settled down to wait. We did not expect much action until about noon or early afternoon, as from experience we had found the middle part of the day was best for sharks and the early morning and evening were often slack periods.

There is always the temptation when nothing is happening for long periods to indulge in a little bottom fishing to while away the time. This is fatal as I have found to my cost. When a shark run does finally occur, the bottom rods must be reeled in and cleared out of the way. By the time this is done the fish may have dropped the bait or may have taken more than one bait. Either way one is in trouble. If the bottom lines are left out and the fish struck, then the bottom lines are probably fouled by the shark before your colleagues can clear them. Things happen so quickly when a shark takes that the most amazing and time-wasting messes can occur. Far better to stick to shark fishing only and if one does want to while away the

(Opposite) Perhaps rather a slow fighter, but a monk-fish such as this 42-pounder will give the angler plenty to think about in its dour and dogged fight

time then try for garfish.

The rubby-dubby attracts more than sharks. Mackerel, garfish, and many other species swim up the trail feeding on the small pieces of fish falling from the bag. Once while fishing off Clare Island on the west coast of Ireland I enjoyed excellent cod and pollack fishing near the surface from fish that had followed up the rubby-dubby trail. If you watch the trail carefully you often see garfish darting about picking up little pieces of fish. At times you can also see them jumping gracefully out of the water and this often signifies that there is a shark close by.

I like to fish for garfish with a light freshwater spinning rod, fixed spool reel, 3 to 5 lb. b.s. monofilament, and a size 9 hook tied direct to the line. Some anglers prefer to use a small float, but in a fairly fast drift this is unnecessary and a few split shot about 18 inches above the hook to make the bait sink is all that is required. A small piece of mackerel skin is excellent for bait and has the advantage of lasting a long time while taking several fish.

On light tackle garfish put up a wonderful display. They are amazingly fast and jump frequently, leading the angler a merry dance as he tries to keep the fish from becoming entangled in the shark lines. If suitable tackle is used I can recommend this as a sport in its own right and if you have no use for the garfish when caught, do put it back. It earns its release by the sport it has given you and to kill for the sake of killing is a poor reward indeed for its efforts.

An hour and a half had passed and the tide was beginning to ebb hard. Our rubby-dubby trail stretched as a smooth slick of quieter water among the tumbling waves as far as we could see. We had just put out a fresh bag of rubby-dubby and then taken in the old one to refill it when the ratchet of one of the reels screeched suddenly and then stopped before we had time to see which one it was. We watched the floats expectantly. John's, which was in the middle, dipped twice in quick succession and then went under as his reel sang out again with the same electrifying sound.

We all grabbed our rods, Alfie and I to reel in while John knocked off the ratchet on his reel and allowed the shark to take line freely until it was beyond the outer float and then he struck hard to set the hook. His rod arched over and the battle was on.

Alfie and I got our rods and baits in and put them up on the fo'c'sle out of the way and did a quick check to make sure that the deck was clear and that there was nothing loose or in the way. When a big shark comes aboard and thrashes about it can create havoc if the deck is cluttered up with gear and such a situation can prove dangerous for the occupants. The shark made several long runs against controlled pressure from John and each time the fish stopped John leant back into it, pumping hard and giving it no opportunity to rest. Finally it dived deep under the boat and the line had to be man-oeuvred around the stern to prevent it catching on the keel of the boat. John pumped the fish to the surface and it made a few more short dives before it lay exhausted alongside.

I had put on an old leather glove, caught the steel trace and gently drew the fish close while Alfie put in the gaff just above the vent. I got my gaff in near the head and together we lifted the fish over the side. A few hard raps on the snout with a cudgel and the fish lay quiet on the deck. A nice blue weighing about 80 lb. Alfie and I got our baits back into the water while John released the hook link from the main trace leaving the hook to be recovered later. He put on a new link and a fresh bait and in a short time was fishing again. We washed down the deck to clear it of blood and make it safe to stand on.

Half an hour later I had a nice fish which made 95 lb. and shortly afterwards a shoal of five sharks swam right up to the boat passing by our baits without touching them. John fed them a few mackerel at a time to keep them interested while Alfie and I reeled in our baits. We had to take our baits out of the water to drop them to the fish which were right on the surface. I put my reel in free spool, but on the check to prevent an over-run in case a shark took the bait and ran hard. This should also be done to avoid breakage when a shark is brought to the gaff, for if it makes a last desperate effort to escape and the brake is on, the line or rod or indeed both may be broken and the fish lost.

Alfie and I had simultaneous strikes and were both into fish together. I let my fish run a long way while Alfie fought his close to the boat to avoid lines becoming tangled. After his fish was landed I brought mine alongside and as it was only a small blue of about 40 lb. I cut the wire near the hook with wire snips and let it go free.

The hook would do it no harm and it would have little difficulty in getting rid of it. We took every fish from that shoal and had four other fish before we called it a day. Coming home between us we had four nice blues ranging from 80 to 95 lb. and had released six smaller fish.

There is no point in killing small blues just as there is no point in fishing for most blue sharks on heavy tackle. To release a small fish calls for the sacrifice of a hook, but few sportsmen would mind making such a small sacrifice. If the fish has been lip-hooked and is fully played out, it should be possible to lift it aboard without using a gaff and the hook can be recovered or the wire cut close to the hook.

The use of light tackle does create some problems. It may not prove strong enough to hold a really heavy fish, perhaps a porbeagle or mako if you are fortunate enough to hook one, but to use heavy tackle on the slim chance of meeting such a big fish is to sacrifice the sport one can enjoy from the ordinary run of blue sharks.

Professional skippers cater for trippers to a large extent and hire tackle to them for the day's fishing. Naturally they want their tackle to last as long as possible and some novices are notoriously ham fisted and could not be trusted with light tackle. The average run of shark cannot show to advantage when taken on heavy gear and naturally the reputation of shark fishing as a sport suffers. However, even experi-enced anglers sharing a boat sometimes persist in using heavy tackle because the playing and landing of a fish on light gear takes time and those not actually into a fish may object to what to them is a waste of good fishing time. How-ever, if you want sport you must be prepared to fish light even though you may find yourself un-popular.

One final word. Do remember that sharks have very dangerous teeth. I have seen a few nasty accidents happen over the years both when extracting the hook from a seemingly dead shark and when gaffing the fish. The use of a clip to secure the short hook-link to the main trace thus allowing for a quick change of hook links, avoids the risk of having to cut out the hook immediately the fish is landed. When a shark is gaffed and swung in over the side, watch out for its swinging head and snapping jaws. It does not take a big fish to remove a lump of

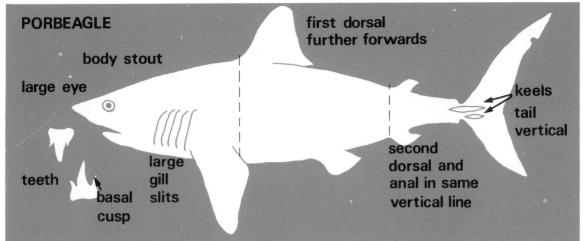

PORBEAGLE

body stout

large eye

first dorsal
further forwards

keels

tail
vertical

teeth

basal
cusp

large
gill
slits

second
dorsal and
anal in same
vertical line

flesh from your hand or leg. In the excitement of the moment one tends to forget and take chances that may turn a day's sport into one of pain and perhaps tragedy.

Blue sharks are not the only species of shark present on our coasts. The basking shark which is a familiar sight on many parts of our coasts at times, is of no angling interest, being a plankton feeder and unlikely to be taken on rod and line. Porbeagle, mako, and thresher sharks have, however, been caught as indeed has the six-gilled shark. Fishing for these species is as yet only in its infancy and a great deal more must be learnt about their distribution, habits, and how best to fish for them before we can expect regular captures to be made. The inability of many anglers to differentiate between the various species has contributed to the lack of reliable information on them, so a brief description here may help in identification.

The blue shark is easily recognisable for it is a long slim shark with a raked-back tail which has a long shallow notch. It possesses long, slender, pointed and sickle-like pectoral fins, the gill slits are small and there are no spiracles. Its teeth are triangular with a serrated cutting edge and are razor sharp. The colour, when the fish is alive, is usually dark blue or marine blue above, shading to white underneath. It does not have a lateral keel on either side of the tail column.

The porbeagle has a thick high body in front, narrowing towards the tail and is in fact a very portly-looking shark. It has large gill slits and the upper lobe of the vertically set tail is larger than the lower. It possesses a larger eye than the blue shark and below the strengthening lateral keel on the tail column there is a small secondary keel which is diagnostic. The teeth are pointed and have small additional basal cusps in the adult fish. The first dorsal fin is much larger

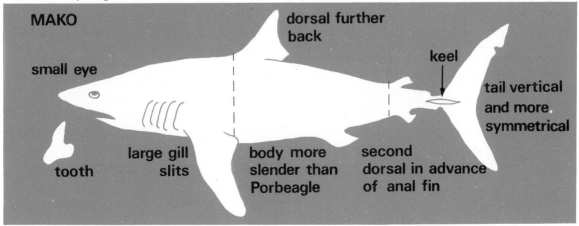

MAKO

dorsal further
back

keel

small eye

tail vertical
and more
symmetrical

tooth

large gill
slits

body more
slender than
Porbeagle

second
dorsal in advance
of anal fin

than in the blue shark and the second dorsal and the anal fin are on the same vertical line. It is usually a greyish or brownish colour on top, shading to white underneath.

The mako shark is a much slimmer and more symmetrical-looking fish than the porbeagle, with a more or less symmetrical tail. The upper lobe of the tail is not noticeably larger than the lower and there is no secondary keel on the tail column, nor are the basal cusps present on the teeth. The origin of the second dorsal is well in

rather like the thresher's and there is a shallow notch in the lower lobe of the tail fin. Its teeth are comb-like and its colour is usually dark brown or blackish.

Back in the early 1930's when Dr. O'Donel Browne and the Marquis of Sligo were pioneering shark fishing at Achill, County Mayo, Ireland achieved quite a reputation for big porbeagle. Dr. O'Donel Browne was an angler and sportsman far in advance of his time and during this period he caught many big por-

THRESHER SHARK

advance of the origin of the anal fin and the colour is usually blue or bluish grey.

Anglers should have no difficulty in recognising the thresher shark because of its very distinctive tail. The upper lobe of the tail is extremely long making up about half of the shark's total length and there is a pit at the root of the tail (which does not have a lateral keel). The second dorsal and the anal fins are very small, but the first dorsal and the pectorals are

beagle, including six weighing over 300 lb. During 1932 he took one of 365 lb. which still stands as the Irish record for the species. Most of his fish were caught in late September and October when shoals of herring were present in the waters off Achill Island. Since then virtually no fishing for porbeagle was done until very recently and it became generally considered that Achill was the only place and late autumn the only time in which to fish for them. A very

SIX-GILLED SHARK

long. The small triangular teeth are not serrated and the colour can be dark grey or bluish grey above and white underparts.

The six-gilled shark is easily distinguished, for as its name implies it possesses six gills. It also differs from the sharks mentioned above in possessing only one dorsal fin while the others others have two dorsals. Its tail is very long

This fine blue shark was caught off the coast of Gibraltar.

different picture, however, is now beginning to emerge.

They appear to be numerous off Devon and Cornwall (the British record which weighed 311 lb. was taken at Looe in 1961) and have been taken on rod and line off the Isle of Man and the Isle of Wight. Clive Gammon has taken them on the Pembrokeshire coast and they have been caught commercially in the North Sea and off East Anglia. In the Irish Sea they have been taken by long-liners and during recent years there has been a commercial long-line fishery for porbeagle shark off the south and south-west coasts of Ireland. This was carried out by a fleet of Norwegian trawlers and large catches were made. The fishing ceased when the market price fell below an economic level.

In Ireland porbeagle have been taken on rod and line on the south, south-west, west, and north coasts in places as far apart as Kinsale, Dingle, Liscannor, Galway, Achill, Killybegs, and Moville in County Donegal. The species appear to be more tolerant of cold water than the blue shark and has been taken close inshore as early as the middle of May and there is evidence that they are off Achill as late as December. They may in fact be present on our coasts for most or all of the year.

They seem to be most plentiful on the west coast of Ireland. Large shoals have been observed off the Clare coast and in the mouth of Galway Bay and it is in this area that most fish have been taken during the last few years. The majority of the fish taken have been small—in the 70 to 120 lb. class. While really big fish have been encountered none have been landed principally because outside of County Clare and in Galway Bay, where a little specialised fishing has been done, most porbeagle have been taken by anglers fishing for other species on tackle which was inadequate for large shark. Furthermore, the usual blue shark technique of drifting using rubby-dubby does not seem to be the answer.

In Liscannor Bay, County Clare, anglers fishing for porbeagle find that they catch more fish when trolling than when drifting using rubby-dubby. If they fish on the drift they find that to be successful the drift must be fast. If it is not fast enough then they use the engine to speed things up a little. The porbeagle has a very large eye, much larger than either the blue or the mako, and it is possible that it may hunt more by sight than scent. This may explain the reduced efficiency of the rubby-dubby technique. Secondly it has been found that porbeagle seem to have a definite 'beat' or 'run' in this area and outside this beat few fish are taken. It also appears that they can be present in shoals and at other times they may move off the coast for a short while.

Dr. O'Donel Browne's technique was to anchor off Mytoege Point, outside Keem Bay in Achill, and bottom fish for such species as red sea bream. Porbeagle were known to frequent this area and when he found some of his hooked fish being chopped by shark he then changed to his heavy shark tackle and fished for porbeagle. Most of his fish were taken close inshore, right under the cliffs at times and this seems to be a feature of porbeagle fishing.

In the Liscannor Bay area the bulk of the fish are taken close inshore in relatively shallow water, 10 fathoms or less. A very accomplished local angler, Jack Shine, of Moy, Lahinch, County Clare, shore fishes for porbeagles from the rocks at Green Island south of Lahinch and also at Ballyrean near Black Head at the entrance to Galway Bay. He has taken quite a number of good fish weighing up to 145 lb. over the last few years and believes that they can be taken on many parts of this coast where there is deep water close in. At Green Island there is a depth of six fathoms close in with deeper water outside. To take fish of such a large size from the shore is quite a remarkable feat and calls for a great deal of patience and perseverance. Conditions must be right for this kind of fishing and there may be long periods—weeks or even months, before the shark are close enough in, and there in good numbers. Inevitably a good many of the fish met with are not landed.

In Galway Bay the porbeagles are also taken in fairly shallow water in places no more than five or six fathoms deep. Quite a number are taken on very small baits—lasks or slips of mackerel fished right on the bottom. In Liscannor Bay, while whole mackerel are used, porbeagle are also taken on small baits as well. Most of the fish are caught near the surface on baits which are trolled about 30 or 40 yards behind the boat. It is interesting to note that Clive Gammon, when fishing off the Welsh coast during the summer of 1967, also found that the porbeagle were close inshore in shallow water. While fishing well offshore in deep water he found that only blue shark were taken, but when the drift took him close inshore into shallow water of less than 10 fathoms the blues were no longer present and porbeagle were taken instead.

The porbeagle is a much stouter fish than the blue shark and is quite on the portly side. Indeed small porbeagle can well be likened to fat little pigs and are quite attractive fish. They weigh far heavier than the blues. A fish measuring five feet with a girth of three feet weighed 130 lb., while an eight foot blue shark would weigh roughly between 110 to 115 lb. They fight quite differntly too. The porbeagle is a stronger fish which fights harder and for longer than the blue shark. It makes shorter, but more powerful runs and fights close to the boat usually circling it many times. In the end it fights in tight circles right under the boat and great care must be taken to make sure that the line is not cut by the keel or the side of the boat.

While the tackle used for porbeagle is basically the same as that used for blue shark it must of necessity be stronger. We are dealing with a more powerful and heavier fish and a rod with more 'backbone' than that indicated for blues is called for. Lines too, need to be stronger. A skilled angler using 60 lb. b.s. line could cope with a reasonable porbeagle provided he had plenty of it, but until more is learned about this form of fishing 80 lb. b.s. line is safer. A large

capacity reel, size 6/0 at least, is necessary and the trace must be of heavy-gauge wire, preferably at least 400 lb. b.s.

Most of the failures by anglers fishing in Galway Bay during the last two years were caused by traces that were too weak, being either broken or cut through. Many traces made of very heavy wire were actually bitten through and this perhaps could be avoided if the short hook-link was made of a single-strand heavy-gauge stainless steel wire.

Hooks should be strong and must be sharp. The porbeagle has a very tough mouth into which it is very difficult to drive home a hook, though this seldom seems to be a problem when it takes a bait which is trolled. Possibly the speed of the bait as it travels through the

A catch of good-sized monkfish taken in shallow water at Fenit, County Kerry

water when trolled helps drive the hook home and of course the take is positive when this method is used. Most difficulty seems to arise when the bait is float fished. It is quite common for a porbeagle to mess about with the bait for long periods without a run developing and even when one does, the fish is not hooked because it has not taken hold of the bait properly.

It is curious that so many of the porbeagle taken on our coasts have been caught in shallow inshore waters where in places at least they seem to be quite numerous. The commercial long-line fishing carried out by the Norwegians was at distances of 10 to 50 miles (but generally 15 to 25 miles) off the Irish coast so that it would appear that their distribution is very wide indeed. Furthermore it was once considered that to catch porbeagle one should look for rough ground or large reefs and fish deep for them. Yet the commercial fishery was one of floating long-lines and most of the fish were caught in the top five fathoms. Many of the porbeagle taken on rod and line in recent years were caught on clean ground, i.e. in Galway Bay.

There is so much which remains to be found out about their habits, haunts, and the best techniques to use. It seems obvious that trolling, a branch of the sport for so long ignored in these islands, though widely used for shark and game fish species in other parts of the world, will play a more important role. Porbeagle fishing in the British Isles is still in its infancy, but I feel sure that before long the problems involved will be solved and shark fishing made more exciting.

Recently, areas previously unfished for shark have sprung into prominence, e.g. off the Isle of Wight and Newhaven. In August 1972 two anglers caught shark some 20 miles off Newhaven and qualified as S.A.C.G.B. members.

While the remaining sharks to be discussed, i.e. the mako, thresher and six-gilled shark, have all been taken on rod and line in our waters, on the whole their capture has been mostly accidental. The mako shark takes us into the realm of big game fishing, for it is considered to be one of the most sporting fish in the sea.

In tropical waters fish exceeding 1,000 lb. in weight have been landed and the British record stands at 500 lb., taken off Eddystone Light. A mako weighing 352 lb. was taken from Looe in 1955 and since then several fish of over 400 lb. have been caught by anglers and some heavy fish have been boated in the Channel Islands.

The only captures in Irish waters were made at Kinsale, County Cork, but mako have also been hooked at both Ballycotton and Dungarvan on several occasions, but unfortunately not landed.

What evidence we have would indicate that it is a summer visitor to our shores and may be found off the south coast of Cornwall, around the Channel Islands and the south coast of Ireland. However, we do not really know. There have been so many reports from various parts of the Irish coast, particularly the west coast, of 'leaping fish' which are almost certainly mako shark, that they may be more widely distributed than we think at present.

Until we evolve more effective methods of fishing for them we will not be in a position to know and here again as in porbeagle fishing we may have to rely heavily on American and New Zealand experience. In these countries mako are taken mostly by trolling with a whole fish or deep drifting with live bait and we will have to experiment with these methods and evolve our own if we are to be more successful.

The same applies to the thresher shark which is again a summer visitor to our waters and seldom taken by anglers. In warmer waters this species can attain weights of 900 lb. or more and the British record stands at 280 lb. and was taken off Dungeness in 1933. It feeds on small shoal fishes such as mackerel, pilchard, and herring, and in summer has been seen on many parts of the coast as far apart as the Orkneys in the north and Kinsale and the Sussex coast in the south. At times it seems quite plentiful off the coasts of Kent and Sussex.

While the thresher shark is mainly a surface and sub-surface feeder and when caught has been taken near the surface, the six-gilled shark has been taken mostly on the bottom. In recent years a small number, two or three fish annually, have been taken in Ireland at Ballycotton, Kinsale, and in Dingle Bay. Most of the fish landed have been small i.e. 80 to 150 lb. in weight but it can attain a very large size. There is a record of a specimen taken at Polperro in Cornwall in 1846 which measures 26 ft. 5 in. in length. The Irish Specimen Fish Committee have, commencing in 1969, opened up a category for this species on their list of fish eligible for awards in order to learn something more about its presence and habits in Irish waters.

Dick Orton

Rods and Tackle

The period since the end of the last war has seen a transition from natural to synthetic raw materials. In 1946 the built-cane fishing rod was dominant for all types of angling. Rods made from a combination of whole cane and lance-wood; whole cane and greenheart; whole cane and built cane were still made in large numbers for bottom fishing. Although greenheart fly rods were on the way out, these were not yet quite defunct, and sea rods made from this material were still to be found on display in all coastal tackle shops. Today however, although numerous trout fly rods are still made from built cane and there are some built cane spinning and bottom rods in circulation, glass fibre has largely taken over both the latter functions, and almost all sea rods are now produced from this material. Built cane was first developed in the U.S.A. before the turn of the century, and at its best is a beautiful rod-building material. The only material which is truly suitable for the manufacture of split cane is Tonkin poles. The best Tonkin grows in a very restricted area of South China which is now, unfortunately, on the wrong side of the Iron Curtain. There are a number of different bamboo canes growing in many parts of the East, and in fact some can be grown in Southern Europe and the warmer parts of Southern England, but generally they do not have the necessary toughness and elasticity which is required for fishing rods, and all attempts to use them have resulted in failure. Only those specimens of *Arundernaria amabilis* found in relatively small areas in South China are entirely suitable.

Analytical examination reveals that this cane consists of parallel, longitudunal hard fibres which are set in a substance of which pectin is the vitally important ingredient. All is protected by a skin of even greater strength and hardness. Exposure to carefully controlled heat solidifies the pectin and enhances still further the natural toughness and elasticity of the material.

Heating is the very first process in built cane rod making, and was originally done over an open gas jet, but the risk of charring and irreparably damaging the valuable surface fibres was considerable. Therefore, this heat treatment is now carried out in ovens. It is commonly, but erroneously thought that the 'baking' is done merely to remove surplus moisture. Although this happens, it is the treatment of the pectin which is the important process. It is, in a sense, akin to the jelling of jam which is achieved by boiling.

After heat treatment, the tonkin pole is cut into sections prior to tapering and cementing. All varieties of cane are harder on the surface than in the centre, and the cane building process is designed to take sections from only the hardest part of the pole, rejoining them to achieve the greatest strength for the minimum of weight. Built cane rods are almost invariably hexagonal in section, a shape which is created by six tapering triangular segments, each with the carefully preserved skin on the outside; planed to shape on a special-purpose machine with cutters which require frequent re-grinding – a fact which is a tribute to the toughness of the material they are processing. Every nine inches or so along the cane, there is a calloused ring which forms knots in the cut material. The knots are ground down, and in the matching of sections care is taken to avoid more than two knots coming together at any one point, as they are a potential source of weakness. Next the sections are cemented together, bound with twine and left to cure.

Section of built cane rod showing six-strip construction

For many years animal glue was used, and it performed its task well, but plastic cements are now used, and when set, may be even harder than the actual cane. The chief arts in cementing lie in achieving even distribution and a perfectly straight blank, which is then stood for some weeks to cure. When animal glue was used the curing process took months! The blanks are then carefully scraped down to remove twine and cement and care is taken to prevent damage to the skin, after which they are ready for further processing. As the rest of the rod-making processes are quite similar, irrespective of the basic raw material, it would be as well now to consider the manufacture of glass fibre blanks.

During the 1939–45 war, glass fibre and synthetic resins were used in aircraft construction in the United States, and the Shakespeare Company, which was involved in this work, saw the possibility of using these materials for fishing rods. The high tensile strength and flexibility of the material seemed promising and subsequently successful experimental rods were built.

Glass fibre fishing rod blanks fall into three general categories, phenolic hollow, solid, and 'Howald process'. The phenolic type have many of the properties of built cane, but are a little lighter for any given strength. Solid blanks are exceptionally strong, almost indestructible in fact, but are heavier and are not at all suitable for rods where length, stiffness and lightness are important. Consequently, one does not see fly rods over $7\frac{1}{2}$ ft. or bottom rods over 8 ft. in length successfully built from this material.

Hollow glass fibre is made by coating woven glass cloth with synthetic resin, wrapping it round a tapered steel rod called a mandrel and then curing it in a hot oven to set the resin. The 'action' of the rod blank is influenced by the gauge and taper of the mandrel, the gauge and weave of the glass fibre cloth, the form of wrapping and the type of synthetic resin used.

Solid glass fibre rod blanks are made from longitudinal glass fibres embedded in resin. Broadly speaking, the more glass fibre there is in proportion to the resin, the better will be the performance of the rod. This is the main factor which influences the widely differing prices of superficially similar solid glass rods.

Dr. Howald working under the auspices of the Shakespeare Company, some years ago, developed a process by which hollow glass fibre rods could be produced from longitudinal fibres instead of woven cloth. Such rods have all their tensile strength in precisely the correct place, with no idle fibres serving only as added weight.

It is obvious that by this process weight can be significantly reduced for any required strength.

However, what is less obvious to the layman is the facility this method of construction affords for sophisticated manufacturing processes. For example: tapering to produce very precise actions in fly and spinning rods. A Howald process rod can be hollow at the butt with minimum wall thickness, progressing to a completely solid tip where reinforcement is desirable.

Howald process blanks can be recognised by spiral marks on the surface of the glass. This gave rise at one time to the misconception that some form of spiral wound glass cloth had been employed. Nothing could be further from the truth.

Prior to curing the blank is wound with cellophane which is afterwards removed. This leaves superficial spiral markings which cannot be removed without damaging the vitally important surface fibres. They therefore remain, and are useful in that they identify the product in an unmistakable manner.

We have now advanced matters in both built cane and glass fibre to the point of the finished blanks. Both now, with reservations, receive similar treatment.

Rods made from tubular steel and other metals, despite their rather limited sales, must not be overlooked. Their production is in the hands of one British manufacturer at this time

(Top) A five-pound rainbow trout in superb condition. A large capacity reel is essential when dealing with fish of this calibre

(Bottom) Short but sturdy boat rods in action. A long rod in a boat can be a distinct disadvantage and even a danger

and it is difficult to evelute their present significance. They first appeared in 1937, and since then have fluctuated in popularity. I think it would be generally agreed that tubular metals, with their rather fierce actions, make better spinning or bottom rods than fly rods.

The next process in the chain of rod manufacture is the fitting of ferrules. These consist of a socket into which a solid ferrule is placed with a 'push fit'; in this manner the rod is assembled for use.

Suction ferrules

Here matters become a little confused by the Redditch trade practice of terming sockets 'ferrules', and ferrules 'counter ferrules' or just 'counters'. Whatever we call them, provided they are properly made, they are the best known method of connecting rod sections. All manner of alternatives have been tried, screw ferrules, various lock joints made with studs and keyways, and a few fishing rods are even made without ferrules at all, the sections terminating in long matching slanting planes which are positioned together and bound with tape.

Standard joints are made of brass, but we now have hollow glass fibre rods which are made complete, with glass fibre sockets and ferrules as integral parts of the blank. These were first introduced for bottom rods but the principle has since been applied successfully to other types of rod. Now there is available a wide range of rods of this type suitable for fly fishing, spinning, and even heavy beachcasting.

With built cane or hollow glass rods which are jointed in the conventional manner with metal ferrules, one of the main points to inspect is the fitting of the socket to the rod section. The highest standards of craftsmanship demand that small cane splints should be glued to the rod to provide a seating for the lower end of the socket which should have deep serrations filed to a taper. These are finally covered by a silk whipping. The cheap and easy way to attach sockets is to grind away the top of the blank until a fit is achieved, but in so doing the invaluable surface fibres are destroyed and the likelihood of a breakage at the socket or ferrule is greatly increased. Therefore mistrust a built cane rod on

which the socket is not of a slightly greater diameter than the cane which is immediately below it.

Virtually all modern fishing rods have cork handles which are usually built by fitting a series of cork bungs on to the butt. These are cemented into place and then machined to a pleasant and convenient shape. The reel fitments are either a pair of sliding tapered rings or a more elaborate arrangement of tapped rings which screw up a threaded metal body. To protect the handles they are finished off at the butt with a metal cap, and finally a rubber button, which somehow succeeds in looking right even though it has little or no functional value.

The rings through which the line passes are attached by silk or terylene whippings, usually in bright and cheerful colours, over which coats of varnish are applied. This gives a final waterproof protection to the natural materials, but merely enhances the appearance of synthetics.

Now we come to the vexed question of intermediate whippings. It is quite incorrect to claim that these do not affect the action, but neither are they functionally necessary. The extra stiffness imparted to a rod by close whippings can be better achieved by adjusting the dimensions and tapers in the original design, so close whippings are, in the main, purely decorative.

Screw reel fitting

In days gone by, they may have been used by third-rate makers to remedy the deficiencies of bad tapering and glueing, but the oft-repeated warnings regarding closely whipped rods are now totally obsolete. Some of the most reputable makers whip rods closely because anglers like them that way. The critics of closely whipped rods might just as logically inveigh against motor cars in two tone finish, or striped shirts, or flowered wallpaper. If an angler fancies a closely whipped rod, he pays a price appropriate to the

(Opposite) Netting a grayling caught on float tackle

*Many coarse fish can be caught by fly fishing methods,
here a chub is netted*

extra labour entailed, and presumably enjoys looking at his handsome property; I know I do.

Now let us consider the variety of fishing rods that are available and their particular features. Bottom fishing commands the greatest numerical following, therefore they shall take pride of place.

In length they are usually from $10\frac{1}{2}$ to 14 ft., although shorter special purpose ledgering rods of solid glass fibre are sometimes offered at fairly cheap prices. Bottom rods are identified by their slim build, long cork handles, often up to 32 inches, and plated wire rings of the full stand off type. The latter are used to hold the fine line as clear as possible of the actual rod. This is particularly important during rain when the result of line sticking to a wet rod can mean a reduction of as much as two-thirds of your casting distance.

Stand-off rod ring and lined end ring

The butt and end rings on bottom rods are commonly lined with toughened glass, which usually bears a brand name, for example, Agatine, Aqualite, Amber, Saphrite, etc.

Bottom rods are required to be light and should not normally exceed 12 drams per foot, except in the case of rods specially designed for carp or other exceptionally large fish, where greater bulk may be needed to give increased power. When comparing rods made from the same raw material, the power, by which we mean the pressure which can safely be applied by the rod in the course of fishing, is directly proportionate to the amount of material used and therefore its weight. By adjusting the degree and position of tapers, the shape of the curve in which a rod flexes when under load can be changed. This influences its casting and striking performance.

An absurd pattern of taper could create a weak point, but in general terms power relates very closely to bulk. A well made eleven foot rod of eleven ounces in weight, will inevitably be more

powerful than an equally well made eleven foot rod eight ounces in weight, assuming that both are made from the same basic material.

Bottom rods often have to be stiff to facilitate quick striking, and the need for their extreme length also relates chiefly to striking. By stiff we mean, in this context, a rod with nearly all the flexibility concentrated in the tip. With the float 30 yards, or more, away and the line floating on the surface, and therefore subject to the effects of wind and current, considerable leverage is required to make fast contact with a fish. An 8 ft. rod would not pick up the slack line sufficiently rapidly. Float fishing in deep water with a fixed float also demands a long rod. However, 8 ft. rods can be used more efficiently for legering, because the line and the hook are in pretty direct alignment.

The most dramatic development in bottom fishing rods during the past 20 years has been the introduction of long, stiff, ultra-light and self-ferruled, hollow glass match rods. These are literally a revelation in length/weight/stiffness ratio. They have totally supplanted the match rods made from Spanish reed which is a light, rigid but not very strong cane grown in Spain and the South of France. Prior to 1960 this type of reed was used almost exclusively in this class of rod.

To explain the term 'match rod' briefly, it should be understood that match fishermen have generally concluded that matches are most frequently won by big bags of quite small fish rather than a few larger specimens. This reflects the general state of our Midland and Northern fisheries where match fishing first developed. To catch such fish, a rod must strike very quickly, but it needs a sensitive tip to correspond with the use of ultra-fine lines.

Prior to the fixed spool reel becoming very popular, match rods did not need to be strong. The rod, 12 to 14 ft., was used single-handed in conjunction with a centre-pin reel. The action used to cast light float tackle was gentle, but when a fixed spool reel was used on such a long rod the high frictional resistance to the passage of the line, as it passed up the rod on casting led to double handed 'punch' casting to increase distance by applying more power. This had fatal results on Spanish reed. The lighter the tackle, the greater the effort that was made to punch it into the wind, and more and more reed rods

A 2 lb. 4 oz. brown trout taken on the dry fly. The special fly box with spring lids to the compartments prevents the loss of flies in high winds

(Right) A deep landing net will prevent a fish from jumping to freedom over the rim

came flooding back to the manufacturers, all uniformly broken about two-thirds of the way up the cork handle. The longer the rod, the more rings, the greater the frictional resistance to the line. It follows, therefore, that the shorter bottom rods, $10\frac{1}{2}$ to 11 ft., all other things being equal, cast more efficiently than the longer 13 to 14 ft. type.

Every fishing rod is a compromise between a number of desired attributes, and so one should select a rod carefully for the exact use for which it is required. If your fishing will mostly be in a lake or wide river, three to ten feet deep, populated by roach, chub, bream, perch, etc., of unexceptional size, a $10\frac{1}{2}$ or 11 ft. rod weighing 8 oz. will do very nicely. Such a rod will permit light weights to be cast maximum distances and it is long enough to give good line control. You will also find that it will have sufficient power to handle lines up to 6 lb. breaking strain. However, if the water contains big tench or specimen chub, it may pay you to buy a rod 2 oz. heavier. If the water holds record carp, a rod to handle 15 lb. b.s. line and 1 oz. weights is recommended. Most of the latter rods are today based on Richard Walker's famous Mark IV formula. These have the advantage of performing well when casting light weights due to the cleverly contrived tapers.

When fishing a very deep water, or one which holds relatively small but shy, quick-biting fish, then a 12 to 14 ft. rod is called for, and where the fish run small the lightest rod of that length is the logical choice. Where depth of water and large fish coincide, a 13 ft. hollow glass fibre rod with an above-average wall thickness should prove adequate, for although it may be slightly heavier the extra power will more than compensate any additional weight.

Spinning rods may be for single or double handed use, and be from 6 to 10 ft. in length and are made in a wide range of weights. At one end of the scale there are the 4 oz., 7 ft. trout spinners designed for single handed use with a fixed spool reel, two or four pound breaking strain lines, one inch devon minnows or two dram spoons. Conversely there are the 10 ft. long salmon spinners weighing 16 oz., capable of imposing a 3 lb. pull and casting 2 oz. weights.

The freshwater species usually fished for deliberately by spinning are salmon, pike, sea trout, brown trout and perch. How powerful a rod is used for the two former species is dictated partly by the size of the bait to be cast, partly by the fishing conditions and partly by personal fancy.

Early season salmon spinning involves three-inch devon minnows, and high fast water. Mastering a big active springer in these conditions requires the most powerful spinning rod, but by mid-summer when the rivers are lower an 8 ft. rod, fixed-spool reel loaded with 8 lb. b.s. line and a $1\frac{1}{2}$ in. devon minnow will meet the situation. Such an outfit is also highly suitable for sea trout. For brown trout the lightest of spinning rods are used, and that which will handle trout will also be adequate for perch.

This is an opportune moment to quote the formula by which one estimates the correct line for any given spinning or bottom rod. It is calculated by taking the maximum load the rod will apply, expressed in pounds, and multiplying by six. The load can be tested on a spring balance, but reputable manufacturers quote the vital statistics for their spinning and bottom rods. Thus, a 16 oz. salmon rod with the power to impose a 3 lb. pull is lined, theoretically, with an 18 lb. line. In practice it will handle 15 to 20 lb. lines happily; use it with a 10 lb. line and a savage taker may break the line; use 30 lb. line and if you hold a well-hooked fish too hard you may break the rod, but usually of course, the hooks tear out of the fish. Specialist fishing tackle dealers should be able to give sound advice on matching rods, lines and casting weights.

The term 'test curve' is used by some manufacturers to describe the power of a spinning or sea rod. It is calculated by fitting a line to the rod and imposing a sufficient pull to make an angle of 90 degrees between the line and the axis of the butt. This load expressed in pounds is called the test curve. As it does not of itself indicate what weight the rod may cast, or what minimum and maximum line strength it will handle, its general usefulness is open to question.

Today, spinning rods are used almost exclusively with fixed spool or multiplying reels. For the former, a tip action is usual, for the latter a slower, more even action is desirable or 'over-runs' may result. Over-runs will be discussed fully in the section of this book which deals with reels.

All spinning rods have large rings which are often lined with the toughened glass which has now taken the place of the lovely but brittle

(Top) Grayling—a sporting fish that may be taken on fly or float tackle

(Bottom) A specimen monkfish. Heavy and powerful fish like this need sound tackle if they are to be landed

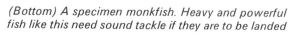

German agate used in years gone by. Double-handed spinners have up to 32 in. handles, but the shorter single handed patterns are likely to have handles of 15 in. or thereabouts. Screw winch fittings are almost standard equipment.

Pike rods represent a separate category, and while all spinning rods other than the very lightest are used for pike, pike fishing may also entail casting heavy live or dead baits, and so rods even more powerful than the heaviest double handed spinner may sometimes be required. Here I would again emphasise that power of rod, strength of line, weight of bait, and size of hooks should all correspond in a logical sequence for any type of fishing. To spin for pike with a 6 oz., 7 ft. rod, 4 lb. b.s. line and a three inch spoon armed with size 3/0 treble hooks is to ask for trouble. The hardness of the pike's mouth makes exceptionally severe demands on the tackle. A 6 oz. rod may be able to drive home a size 10 treble hook on a one inch spoon, but big spoons and plugs with their correspondingly large hooks, measuring that much further from point to barb require 9 or 10 ft. double-handed spinning rods, weighing about 16 oz.

Sea rods are often catalogued as being suitable for casting 6 oz. leads, why then do we not consider such rods as dual purpose, for sea and/or pike fishing? Although this would seem quite rational we do not do so. In this case it is the rate at which the force is applied when making the cast which is the factor to be reckoned with. The shock loading commonly applied when casting a firmly attached 6 oz. sea lead would tear a live bait straight off the hooks. Therefore when pike fishing with live baits the cast is made quite gently and in consequence we may contemplate a much lighter rod. It may be heavier than the heaviest spinner, but it is certainly less than a sea rod. Such a rod will not throw a spinner correctly, neither would it be comfortable for continuous casting. The all-round pike fisher therefore needs at least two rods, one for spinning and one for natural baits. The latter need not be expensive, and will probably be 8 ft. long and constructed from solid glass fibre. It should be capable of imposing a 5 lb. pull and should have rings large enough to allow the passage of a float stop so that a sliding float rig may be used when live baiting in deep water. The ferrule and socket should be proportionately strong, and as even medium-sized pike are quite large fish, the

comfort conferred by a long cork handle when playing one is a great benefit.

Casting a trout fly accurately at long range, presenting it delicately and continuing to do so all day without undue fatigue makes the maximum demand on the skill of both angler and rod designer. Power is needed for distance, but stiffness coupled with weight means wrist strain. Delicacy of presentation and fatigue-free casting are best ensured by a rod with an even progressive action which starts well down the butt. One can feel such a rod moving like a living thing, right down to the grip, but extreme accuracy and fast fly delivery are not its strong points. Such a rod though, with all the dimensions beefed up for power, can throw a very long line indeed, and for reservoir bank fishing in particular, rods of this type have proved very successful. So, it will be seen that while all rods represent a compromise between the many and various desirable but mutually conflicting attributes, the conflict is sharpened to its most extreme form in the case of fly rods. This is largely because of the much greater physical demands made on the angler when fly casting; it rates almost as an athletic pursuit.

There has been controversy over the place hollow glass fibre has in the fly rod picture, and I feel obliged to say quite definitely that personally I have not yet handled a hollow glass fly rod equal in performance to the best of the built cane rods. I have doubts as to whether the properties of man-made materials lend themselves to making really first-rate fly rods, irrespective of tapers, dimensions or wall thicknesses. There always seems to be either an excessive rigidity or an excessive flexibility, often an unhappy combination of both in the same rod. It would be wrong to say that reasonably serviceable and hard-wearing fly rods cannot be made from this material. I do not think we have yet seen the end of important progress in glass fibre fly rods.

An interesting development in fly rod design lies in the treatment of good natural tonkin cane with synthetic resin. Sharpes of Aberdeen have for many years carried out an impregnation process in which blanks are dehydrated and reduced to a jellied consistency prior to bombardment with the type of resin used in glass fibre rod manufacture. Thus a very deep penetration right down into the fibres is achieved with a consequential vast improvement in durability. Actions are sharpened and the working life of the rod increased many times.

The more sophisticated characteristics of a first-rate fly rod go beyond anything words can adequately communicate. To say that there is a steely rigidity coupled with great flexibility is to contradict oneself, but that is how a good cane fly rod feels. Power is given to the rod by wrist and forearm movement, a power the rod seems to multiply by its own innate virtue.

Fly fishing sub-divides into wet and dry fly. Wet flies are usually used three on a cast, dry flies singly. When fishing a team of wet flies in a gusty wind, (and when and where in Great Britain is there not likely to be a gusty wind?) horrible tangles are an ever-present menace and a rod which casts a wide entry loop is to be preferred to one casting a narrow entry loop. Rods with even, slow, easy actions cast wide entry loops, and so such rods are to be preferred for wet fly fishing. As it is usual when fishing a wet fly to cover the water methodically, rather than to cast to a particular rising fish, the lack of extreme accuracy inherent in the slow actioned rod is not critically important.

Three spaced flies require at least a three yard nylon cast, and so wet fly rods tend to be fairly long—9 to 10 ft. is usual, although 10½ to 11 ft. and even 11½ ft. single handed fly rods are still traditionally used in some parts of Scotland for loch fishing.

1. Wide entry loop   2. Narrow entry loop

Dry fly rods built to cast a single fly are less flexible and shorter, 8 to 9 ft. The stiffest dry fly rods of all are built in the United States and are just rigid poles with flexible tips. Their fly delivery is very fast and very accurate over short distances. As many anglers, particularly at the beginning of their fly fishing careers, like to make one rod serve for everything, manufacturers make fly rods which are a compromise between the two extremes. These are usually 8½ or 9 ft. long, described as having 'midway' actions, and are often quite nice fly rods, and fulfil all that is claimed for them.

Great versatility is demanded from a fly rod used in the conventional way. One minute it is required to present a fly delicately to a fish rising 5 yards from the angler; ten minutes later he may be trying to force out 25 yards of line into the wind, fast enough to cover a feeding fish before it moves out of range. All this makes considerable demands on the designer.

The designing and building of fly rods is an art which is not acquired in two or three years, and for this reason alone the public should be suspicious of cheap models. It is not necessary to pay the highest prices on the market to obtain a decent article, but the cheapest leave much to be desired.

Trout fly rods are almost always single handed, with a short handle 8 to 12 inches long, and a screw winch fitting at the very bottom. Low bridge rings are usual, with imitation agate butt and end rings. The end ring must be large enough to pass the double tapered line appropriate to the rod, and this is a point to note when buying a new fly rod. Ferrules and sockets should be a tight fit, as the stresses peculiar to fly casting tend to force the upper joints round in the sockets so that the rings get out of alignment. When, during fishing, it gradually becomes harder to cast the distance intended, this is the first point to check.

Fly rods as short as 6½ or 7 ft. are made for fishing small overgrown brooks, where the trees often meet overhead and make casting with a rod of orthodox length virtually impossible. Such rods are built for very light lines, and should not be used with heavier ones. Size HEH is usual. In

(Opposite) A secure screw reel fitting and a comfortably shaped cork handle make the catching of such fish on a fly rod that little bit more enjoyable

fly casting, it is the line itself which provides the casting weight, and so the match between rod and line is critical. The match between fly rod and reel, to which so much importance was attached by writers in the past, is now hardly relevant. Some fly reels are better than others, but all that I know are at least of reasonable lightness in weight.

Underlining a rod prevents its power being developed properly, and leads to a sense of frustration as proper distance cannot be reached and much effort is wasted in trying to remedy this by brute force. Overlining makes casting easier in the first instance, but the line goes out of control very easily and may fall low on the back cast which, if there are obstructions behind, may lead to disaster. The rod also wears out more quickly and may even break under the strain of trying to maintain control over a long aerialised line of too great a weight. The onus is on the manufacturer and dealer to make honest and intelligible recommendations.

Much of what applies to trout rods applies also to salmon fly rods, but these are stouter, longer (10½ to 14 ft.), and double handed. Salmon fishing with the fly sub-divides into early season fishing with large flies and sunken line, in which a double handed rod 12 to 14 ft. in length is employed, and summer fishing with a floating line and a small very lightly dressed fly. This is termed 'greased line' fishing and is usually done with a shorter rod, 10 to 11½ ft. single or double handed and built with a stiffer action for line mending, i.e. lifting the floating line as it drifts downstream and flicking it upstream to avoid dragging the fly. It is interesting to note that two generations ago salmon rods were as much as 18 ft. in length.

On the River Spey, where high banks make conventional casting difficult or even impossible,

A heavy-duty boat rod in action, it is fitted with roller rings to reduce line friction

(Opposite) A Kennet barbel. Strong tackle is needed to handle these fish and waders can sometimes help in reaching awkward swims

a type of switch cast has been developed in which the line remains in front of the angler all the time but this imposes such enormous strain on the rod that a normally ferruled rod cannot be used. They shear off at the sockets. It is for this style of ffshing that the spliced rods referred to earlier are made. The joints are bound together with tape, and the stresses are thus distributed more evenly.

As the use of the second hand more than compensates for the extra 30 or 40 per cent in length, the action of a salmon rod is not usually considered quite so critical as that of a trout rod. Nevertheless, in working back towards the surface, and ultimately lifting 30 or 40 yards of line, the rod is subjected to great strain so smoothness of action is to be desired in order to distribute these strains as evenly as possible. Also, in tribute to these exceptional requirements, some form of lock joint ferrule is not necessarily an anachronism in the case of a salmon rod. This is one of those areas where opinions may genuinely differ. Some manufacturers believe they can make plain suction ferrules accurately enough for the job, others prefer the safeguard of a locking device.

Last, but certainly not least, we come to salt-water rods. Many of the fish caught by sea anglers are no larger than the better class fresh-water bream, tench and chub. Nevertheless, very much stouter tackle is generally used, which is due entirely to the effect of the tides. When these are ebbing or flowing, the moving water creates such power that the sea angling novice, one possibly brought up on freshwater fishing, can hardly credit the evidence of his senses.

In the fast reaches of a powerful river, a $1\frac{1}{2}$ oz. leger lead of the right shape will hold the bottom. I have had an 8 oz. lead picked up and rolled towards France like a marble by the tide off Deal pier. The pull was such that line was drawn from the reel against the tension of the check. What happens, therefore, when even a three pound bass turns his flank broadside to the run of the tide can be imagined. Thus, while the tip of a really stout salmon spinning rod which has been built to kill 30 pounders may measure a mere $\frac{3}{16}$ in. in diameter, the tip of a 10 ft. beachcaster which may never have to kill a fish over 5 lb. in weight in ten years' use, is likely to measure $\frac{5}{16}$ in. in diameter at the tip and to be built up in proportion all the way down!

The main sub-divisions in salt-water rods are beach or surfcasters, boat rods, and the general purpose rods which are used off piers and jetties.

Beachcasters, 9 to 12 ft. in length, are designed for casting heavy leads very long distances. Some are built with most of the action in the tip, some with springy butts. Both seem to me to work very well, and there are certainly keen protagonists for each school of thought. Handles should be long enough for the angler to space his hands widely, and a screw winch fitting made preferably from plated brass is essential. The position of this is important, and as most beach fishermen use multiplying or fixed spool reels, the best position is well up the handle with just a single hand grip in front for comfortable retrieve.

Sockets and ferrules should be made from materials as strong as the rod. Rings on all sea rods are a vexed question, the abrasion is terrific, and so of course is corrosion, but the metals which best resist abrasion do not necessarily have the highest resistance to corrosion. Rings are usually mounted in cradles which in turn provide feet for attachment to the rod, the rings being fixed by welding or brazing into the cradles. The point of the attachment between ring and cradle is a focus for electrolytic action, a major source of all salt-water corrosion.

Finally, as sea rods take a deal of hard wear, the rings must be shatterproof. This almost rules out non-metallic substances. By and large, I think the task of providing adequate rings on sea rods has given manufacturers more headaches than any other single problem. Today, improved plating processes, the availability of a more versatile range of stainless steels, and the development of a very hard resilient pink ceramic material means that sea rod rings are greatly improved. I would, however, hesitate to use the word 'infallible'.

As with other rods, matching the tackle is vitally important. Tides vary around the coast, and rods to cast up to 2, 4, 6, or 8 oz. leads are on sale. Obviously, a man who always fishes a beach where a 2 oz. lead will hold bottom does not wish to encumber himself with a great stout rod that has been built to cast 8 oz. It is important to select the rod for the exact job it has to do.

The really big sea fish, and they may weigh over a hundred pounds, are almost invariably caught by boat anglers well off shore, e.g. shark,

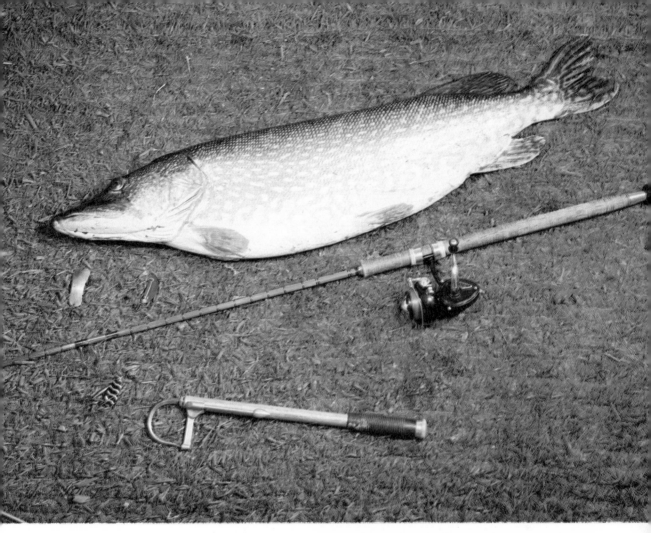

An 18 lb. pike taken on spinning tackle. The telescopic gaff helped make sure of its capture

(Right) An assortment of Devon minnows

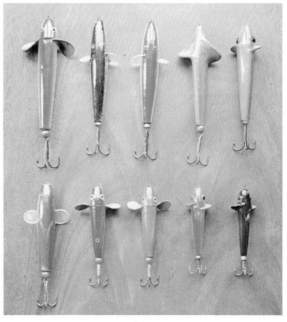

tope, skate and conger are some of the big species hunted by the boat fishermen. Rods for shark and skate may well taper from $\frac{3}{4}$ in. above the handle to $\frac{3}{8}$ in. at the tip and this in only 6 ft. of length. Such rods can impose a pull of over 20 lb. and carry a line of 120 lb. b.s. Coaxing a 200 lb. skate off the bottom may demand all that this tackle can give and in the process reduce a strong man to a shaking, sweating wreck in 20 minutes. Happily, he is likely to recover quite rapidly!

An example of a modern hollow glass fibre rod and multiplier reel and the fish that may be caught by the correct use of well-designed tackle

Boat anglers also fish for smaller species, e.g. pollack, cod, etc., where 10 and 20 pounders respectively are very good fish, therefore lighter boat rods are also in demand. All boat rods are short, as casting is not involved, and safety in the boat is a factor not to be ignored. Boat rods are usually made from a one-piece blank let into a socket in the handle of the rod and are from $4\frac{1}{2}$ to $6\frac{1}{2}$ ft. in length. A good stout brass screw winch fitting is essential.

Little need be said of general purpose sea rods except that they are usually 7 to 9 ft. in length and may have to throw just as heavy leads as beach rods. As stated, almost all sea rods are now made from solid or hollow glass fibre. Solid glass is very good for the shorter rods, and comparatively inexpensive. Hollow glass is lighter but dearer, although the price gap is closing fast.

(Opposite) The end of the battle and the strain is off both tackle and angler. A twenty pound pike is proudly displayed

There is a stretch of coastline in the South-west, just over 100 miles from end to end as the gull flies but probably three to four times that distance as the shoreline winds, where tides are slack and the rods in vogue are little different from powerful freshwater patterns. A rod suitable for float fishing for pollack and mackerel may be made from the same blank as a double handed salmon spinner, albeit fitted differently, while the angler who spins for bass may use a $7\frac{1}{2}$ ft. rod which would be just as suitable for sea trout in a Welsh river. All that has already been said of spinning rods is relevant, but in addition it should be appreciated that a fresh-water spinning rod may not have had its fittings proofed against salt-water corrosion. As aluminium alloys are specially vulnerable, watch this point closely when buying a light spinning rod for salt-water use.

Finally, a word of warning regarding heavy built cane sea rods. Some of these which come in from abroad are little more than rubbish. Before buying, test them by flexing and always make sure that the rod straightens correctly. If it does not, it is not strictly speaking a fishing rod at all, and is desperately poor value, however low the price may be.

Terry Thomas

Salmon and Sea Trout

Fishing is to no small extent a matter of applied natural history. The more you know about your quarry, the better chance you must have of interpreting its moods, and ultimately of catching it. Let us then start by considering briefly the life history of the salmon.

Salmon

The 'King of Fish' is anadromous—that is it spends a considerable period of its life in the sea but ascends a river, generally the river where it was born, to spawn. Salmon spawn in winter, generally in late November and early December. The resultant progeny usually spend two years in freshwater. These are termed 'parr' and are small, trout-like, aggressive fish which grow to a length of only a few inches. Then, usually in April or May they feel the urge to migrate. A chemical change in their body gives them a silvery sea-going coat and they become known as smolts. They set off to the sea, generally in shoals, and disappear into its vastness. Until only a few years ago we had no idea where they went. Now we know that many journey all the way to Greenland waters.

The average salmon spends about two years in the sea. Some spend rather less time and are known as grilse. These rather different salmon, slimmer, smaller and with forked tails, mostly appear in our rivers in summer. Really big fish, 25 pounds and more, spend an extra year or two in salt water. During this period in the sea they feed continuously on a rich selection of foods and grow at a rapid rate.

After two years in a river they weigh only a few ounces: after the same period in the sea they will weigh anything between seven and twenty pounds.

Salmon ascend rivers at different times of year. Early rivers, like the Tweed, Wye, and Tay, have a 'spring' run – spring in this case often meaning the bitter days of January and February. 'Springers' are frequently big fish. Most rivers have a summer run and some have an autumn run, again often including big fish which have had an extra few months of sea feeding. As we shall see, these fish behave rather differently, but all have one thing in common; when they approach fresh water they cease feeding and their digestive organs shrink to a degree which makes feeding impossible. There is no doubt about the fact that salmon do not feed in rivers. If they did, in no time at all, every small living creature would be eaten.

Throughout the whole period in fresh water they live on the vast store of energy they have built up in the sea. They also nurse their strength by resting in between journeys further and further up the river in 'lies' where they are able to maintain themselves with a minimum of effort.

Most salmon lies are known and have been known for centuries. These energy saving holts can in some cases be pinpointed to within inches. 'See yon black boulder', the local will say. 'Six inches this side is the taking place'. Most lies are more generally described–'from that grassy point down to the hawthorn', or, 'wade in at the neck of the pool and fish right down to the fence'.

There is a point when a lie ceases to be a lie

A running sea trout summons all the power and strength that its lithe body contains in an effort to continue its upstream journey past a weir

*A north-country sea trout caught from the River Tyne.
These larger fish normally run later in the season after
the smaller shoal fish have entered the rivers*

and becomes 'holding water'—an area likely to
contain fish.

Lies obviously vary according to the height of
the water. A comfortable resting place in high
water might well be on dry land in low water.
There are in consequence high water lies and
low water lies. So the first lesson learned is that
local knowledge is a great help. The experienced
angler, knowing what salmon require in the way
of comfort, can pin-point holding water even on
a strange river. But only the experience of
catching a number of salmon from one exact
spot gives the necessary knowledge of the exact
taking place.

Salmon proceed up rivers in very different
ways. Some fish, particularly towards spawning
time, arrive at the higher reaches quickly. Others
move much more slowly and others spawn low
down in the main stream. For the most part,
however, salmon try to spawn high up on the
main river and its tributaries and they journey to
these spawning grounds in a series of spurts with
resting periods in between. Generally they run
on high water when the river has risen, usually

due to rain, for the spate enables them to
negotiate obstacles and shallows more easily.
When they become tired, or when the water
drops, they stop their upstream movement and
seek another comfortable resting place.

The best time to catch a salmon is when it has
just taken up residence in a new lie. At this time
it is almost certain to take a properly presented
lure. So the next lesson to learn is the value of
being in the right place at the right time.

As the salmon spends more and more time in
the river living on the store of energy built up in
the sea, its appearance changes. This change is
also due to the development of its reproductive
organs. From the lovely silver-and-blue fish it
was when it entered fresh water, the female becomes darker while the cock fish takes on a
strong reddish hue and often develops a hook at
the end of its lower jaw, which is called a kype.

After spawning most fish die, but a small per-
centage, usually less than ten per cent, survive
and these are mostly hen fish. These survivors
are known as kelts and it is illegal to take them.
In spring they are a nuisance, for they are often
easy to hook and much time is lost playing and
returning them. Many kelts are wasted-looking,
ugly fish. Some, however, are bright handsome
fish and it is often quite difficult to tell a fresh

Fishing down a wooded sea-trout water. The fish are most likely to be found in the deeper, calmer water under the trees on the far bank during daylight

fish from what is called a 'well-mended kelt'.

Here, very briefly, is the story of the salmon, which if nothing else must give rise to the question, why a fish which does not feed in fresh water will take a fly, spinner or other bait. The honest answer is that we do not know, but there are all sorts of theories relating to this behaviour. Let me list some facts and ideas which will give you, initially at least, a right mental approach to salmon fishing.

Fact 1 All its life the salmon is a predator, preying on other creatures.

Fact 2 When the adult salmon enters the river it spends a great deal of its time rather like a hibernating animal, in a sort of trance. In this way it conserves energy. At times, however, it wakes up and is very active. This activity is frequently, but not always, connected with a rising river which enables it to move upstream.

Theory 1 Activity is strongly connected with the availability of oxygen to the fish.

Fact 3 The level of activity varies greatly in intensity, but it is during these periods that the latent predatory instinct of the salmon is aroused

and it will take fly or spinner. There are occasions when this instinct is aroused to a very strong degree and salmon all over the river become easy to catch. More often, alas, the fish merely reaches a stage when it will possibly take a fly or lure.

Theory 2 (Although this is almost a fact.) Under these more common circumstances a salmon will take a fly or spinner which at that moment looks like and behaves like some natural creature. This is what salmon fishing is all about and we will discuss this in detail when we deal with methods.

Finally, a word about rivers. There was a time when salmon entered all, or nearly all the rivers in this country. Now pollution and other factors have reduced the number up which they run. The salmon has two needs in a river. It must be reasonably clean and well oxygenated and it must have good gravel beds into which eggs can be laid.

For the most part these two requirements are only found in rivers which rise in hilly country. Most rivers in the West Country have a run of salmon, as do all unpolluted rivers in Wales, the North, Scotland, and Ireland. The chalk streams which enter the English Channel from Portsmouth westwards to the Somerset border are all

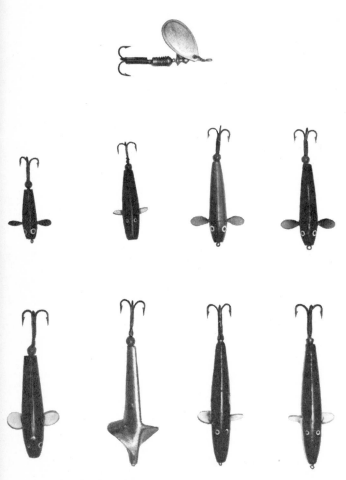

A selection of successful Devon Minnows and lures for salmon spinning

are similar and the resultant small fish spend the same amount of time in the river before migrating to the sea. After a few months in coastal waters it returns to the river in summer in shoals of small, silver, incredibly game fish called finnock or herling. At this stage it is the equivalent of the grilse and displays similar relative strength, speed, and leaping ability.

Although sea trout, particularly the very big ones (a big sea trout for Britain is one of between eight and twenty pounds) run early in the year, in some rivers as early as spring salmon, they are for the most part summer fish. Most sea trout enthusiasts start to become excited as June approaches. The smaller fish tend to shoal, but as they grow bigger, as always happens with shoal fish, they become more solitary. Unlike the salmon they are less dependant on lies and move around a great deal, particularly when on the feed.

The behaviour of sea trout varies a great deal. In the West Country, for example, and on some Welsh rivers, it is extremely difficult to catch them during the day and most fish are caught in the dark. However in the west of Ireland, in lochs in Ireland and Scotland, and on rivers like the Lune, they behave like brown trout and can be caught in the light as well as in the dark.

Like salmon, sea trout use high water to travel up the river, but at times they do run in very shallow water. During the day they pick if possible, a shady lie under trees, under rocks, under the bank, and at times in underwater rat holes.

Their distribution is similar to the salmon, but more widespread. There are few unpolluted rivers in Britain which are not visited by at least a few sea trout. They also ascend small streams which would not be big enough to hold salmon. In river systems which include lochs, sea trout sometimes remain for long periods and some of the best fishing is in waters of this kind.

Sea trout have many local names. In Ireland they are called 'white trout'—a very descriptive name. Their Welsh name is 'sewin' and in the West Country they are called 'peel'. On menus they frequently appear as 'salmon trout'. Finnock are sometimes called 'whitling' and, in the north-west, 'sprods'.

A beautiful stretch of salmon and sea trout water is the River Ewe at Poolewe in North-West Scotland.

salmon rivers. Salmon will also spend time in lakes and lochs on their way to the spawning grounds, but must eventually ascend feeder streams, for they can only spawn in running water.

Sea trout

The sea trout is exactly the same fish as the brown trout but behaves like the salmon and spends part of its life in the sea. Where it differs from the salmon is that it does not normally grow as big, it commonly returns to the river to spawn a number of times, and it does not generally travel far out into the ocean. In salt water it is a coastal feeder and, thank goodness, unlike the salmon, it does feed in fresh water.

The start of the sea trout's life is pretty well identical with that of the salmon which I have previously described. The spawning methods

Terry Thomas

Tackle and Casting for Game Fish

Salmon fishing can be divided into three methods: fly, spinning, and bait. The last named has certain limits set on it and I shall not deal with it in great detail. In any case it is practised either with fly tackle or with a spinning outfit.

All types of casting consist of throwing a weight using the spring of the rod. In the case of fly fishing the weight is in the line itself, while in spinning the weight is at the end of the line. The tackle used, therefore, varies greatly and the fly rod is longer and more flexible than the spinning rod.

The rod, or rods, you need for salmon fishing depends on how widely you intend to fish, what rivers you are going to try and of course the depth of your pocket.

Let us first examine what rods the keen salmon angler ought ideally to have. For fly fishing on very big rivers (and some small ones) a 14 ft. strong rod is needed. For all-round work, particularly with a floating line, the best length is between 12½ and 13 ft. For small rivers, where a double-handed rod can be a nuisance, and for very low water work, a single-handed rod, something between 9½ and 10 ft., is an asset. A reservoir rod is just right for this type of fishing. If it has an extension butt, that is a six-inch extension which can be pushed into the bottom of the butt to give a longer handle, this makes the rod more versatile and the playing of a fish more comfortable.

Three rods are also ideal for spinning – a 10 ft. powerful rod for early fishing on big rivers; one a foot or eighteen inches shorter for all-round work; and a seven-foot light rod for use with a fixed spool reel and light line in low water conditions.

To match both the long fly rods a four-inch fly reel is necessary. For reasons we shall deal with when we discuss methods, the 14 ft. rod needs both a sinking line and a floating line, so a spare reel drum is useful. With a battery of rods of this nature we would be thinking only of floating lines for the two other rods. The single-handed rod needs a 3½-inch wide-drum reel.

For the heavy spinning rod you need either a multiplier loaded with 15 lb. breaking strain braided line or a fixed spool reel carrying 12 lb. breaking strain nylon monofilament. For the middle length rod you can again use either of these reels with line three or four pounds lighter while the light rod must have a fixed spool reel loaded with 6 lb. breaking strain line. But this is all advice on equipment which many will not be able to afford, so how do we reduce the battery without losing too much efficiency?

For general salmon fishing go for both middle rods. But, if you have a reservoir fly rod and/or a stiffish seven-foot spinning rod, you can get away with these, particularly on small rivers. When however we deal with methods I shall try to show the advantages of length in a salmon rod.

Now comes the important question of cost. You can pay between £30 and £60 for a salmon fly rod and roughly half these amounts for a spinning rod. It is possible to buy an excellent, but more plainly finished fly rod for about £15 and a similar quality spinning rod for about £10. What you should *not* do is buy either a second-hand rod, or one that is unbranded. Buying a

The single-handed fly cast near completion. The forward power stroke has been completed and the line is turning over to extend in front of the angler

A brace of trout with tackle and an assortment of flies.

A superbly coloured brown trout

fishing rod is like buying a car. The normal production family car will take you from A to B just as well and probably as quickly as a much more expensive model. If, however, you want rather better performance and better fittings, then you pay more.

For the double-handed rod you need a four-inch reel. These cost between £6 and £8, but a second-hand branded reel is a safe buy, particularly if you are mechanically minded enough to assess wear. Alternatively the 3½-inch Intrepid King Size at 45 shillings serves and is ideal with a single-handed rod. Single-handed fly rods strong enough for salmon fishing run from about £8 up to three times that amount.

With regard to spinning reels, a suitable fixed spool reel costs somewhere between £5 and £8 and a multiplier around about £15. I prefer braided line on the latter which costs approximately £1.

Of all the items the fly line is the most important and a modern floater or sinker costs in the region of £5. Nylon monofilament either as a line or for making casts and traces, costs very little. Braided line for use with a multiplier or as backing (that is reserve line to attach to the fly line) costs about £1 per hundred yards. On top of these capital items you need flies and baits, either Devons or spoons, which again we will deal with in detail when we discuss methods. These will cost about three or four shillings each.

The other items to complete the salmon fisher's equipment need cost little. A gaff to land your fish, a bag in which to carry your tackle, scissors, leads, and a loaded stick to despatch the landed fish. Some form of waterproof clothing is advisable and on most rivers a pair of waders is an advantage. On big rivers chest waders provide a number of benefits.

These then, are the bare essentials. Now let us look at how they are used to propel fly or bait to where the salmon lie.

Space prevents my dealing with the problems of casting in detail and the wise reader can study the subject fully by reading either my book, *Casting*, or *The Angler's Cast* by Captain T. L. Edwards and Eric Horsfall Turner. Your public library can provide either or both.

Casting, let me first say, is not an art, as many would have you think, but a matter of applied mechanics.

All you have to cast with is a spring, in the shape of your rod, which is flexed by the weight of either the fly line, or the weight of a spinner and lead. All bad casting comes from the rod not being flexed at all or through its losing flexibility.

Let me assume that you have a double-handed fly outfit, but have never cast a fly in your life. Mount the rod, making sure the rings are in line, fit the reel to the rod butt and thread the

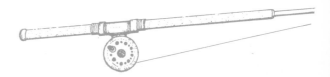

Position of reel on double-handed fly rod

line through the rings, making sure you do not miss one. Tie two or three yards of monofilament to the end of the line, this prevents the line end cracking like a whip.

Make your first efforts on a lawn because on land you can begin by pulling off perhaps twelve yards of line and laying this out in front of you. (Figure 1.) It is easier to cast on water but the first difficult step is to work the line out.

Having pulled the line out, take up the rod holding it lightly at the butt cap with the left hand (taking it for granted you are right-handed) and comfortably high up the butt with the right hand. Put your right foot in front and place as much of your weight on it as you can. Start the cast with the rod roughly horizontal and using mostly your right hand, raise the rod smartly to a position just past the vertical. (Figure 2.) This causes your line to fly over the top of the rod in a loop which you must allow to unroll until the line is fully extended in the air. (Figure 3.) At this point you reverse the procedure, (Figure 4) and if you have carried out the movements correctly the line extends itself in front of you. (Figure 5.)

The all-important position is at the top of the cast. If you can prevent the rod passing beyond the position just past the vertical, you are well on the way to making an efficient cast.

With a single-handed rod follow the same procedure. It is easier to cast with a double-

Double-handed fly casting

handed rod, for there are two hands in control to prevent it moving beyond the vertical position on the back cast. It is more difficult to control the rod when casting single-handed.

Casting with a fixed spool reel is initially easy. Having mounted the outfit, tie a lead of about ¾ oz. on the end of the line. Take a comfortable hold on the rod and reel with the right hand so that the forefinger can encircle the line. Hold the line either in the crook of the forefinger or with the fingertip against the reel spool or the cork of the rod handle. Lift out the bale arm. Then swing the lead in the direction you wish it to go, releasing the line with your forefinger as the lead starts to fly in the required direction. It takes a little time both to find the correct casting arc and the correct timing of line release, but as I

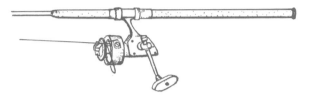

Correctly mounted fixed-spool reel

said, initially it is easy to cast with this type of reel. To get the most out of a fixed spool reel is more difficult. For instance it is essential to be able to control the cast by dropping the forefinger onto the spool lip to slow up or stop a cast.

The multiplier is not easy to use. It is mounted on the double-handed rod and line release is controlled by thumb pressure on the revolving drum. The drum speed also needs controlling during a cast or a tangle results. This can be performed by the thumb although most reels now have governors which help to prevent tangles.

The cast with a multiplier needs to be a long smooth swing and the moment of release is not easy to time. Nevertheless, the multiplier has an important place in salmon fishing, particularly in early fishing, and the trouble taken to master this type of reel is certain to be repaid.

With both types of reel, as progress is made, the caster should concentrate on making his cast

Correctly mounted multiplier reel with rod rings and reel uppermost

as overhead as possible to achieve maximum accuracy.

Sea trout

Sea trout can be caught by all forms of fly fishing, by spinning, and by bait fishing. Sea trout fly rods are still listed in many catalogues, usually being powerful models between 10 and 11 ft. in length. Such rods are quite unnecessary except for specialised use such as sunk-line work using big lures and for use on rivers where very big fish can be expected. The modern reservoir rod is much better for these circumstances and for most sea-trouting a modern trout fly rod between eight and nine feet long is heavy enough, and costs between £8 and £15.

The well-equipped angler needs both a sinking and a floating line and a fly reel which takes plenty of backing. These, the casts, and means of making them plus ancilliary articles are dealt with in his section on reservoir fishing by Dick Orton and there is no point in duplicating his advice. Dick also covers single-handed casting, so again I can devote more space to the different methods of catching sea trout.

Spinning is both a sporting and successful method of catching sea trout. In coloured water they are easily caught on such tackle, but when the water is low and clear there is much skill involved and light tackle is essential. A light spinning rod of the type described for salmon, or rather lighter, which can preferably be used with lines of from 2 to 6 pounds breaking strain, is ideal. A fixed spool reel, again already described, is essential for light baits and fine lines.

Bait fishing, either with a float or by other means is practised on some rivers while on others it is wisely prohibited. Float fishing is a highly skilled art and no one has more admiration for the float artist than I. But this artistry is out of place on a sea trout river. The skilled maggot angler, groundbaiting properly, can butcher quantities of sea trout. So can the worm fisher in a spate. There are better ways of angling for one of the world's great sporting fish and it is on these that I shall concentrate in the following pages.

Waterproofs, waders, and other items for sea trout are as previously described, but there is one item, a stout staff, which is a comfort in the dark when you are wading a river with a difficult bed. A torch, of course, is essential.

Terry Thomas

Salmon Fishing Methods

The methods of catching salmon can be broadly divided into sunk-line fly fishing, floating-line fly fishing, heavy spinning, light spinning, and bait fishing. Each has its own time and place. Again broadly speaking, sunk-line fly fishing and heavy spinning are used when the water is cold and when the river is in spate, and floating-line fly fishing and light spinning are used when it is warm and the river is at, or below, normal level.

Of these methods the sunk line is by far the most difficult. It was my original intention to avoid describing it and to recommend instead, the use of heavy spinning, which is much easier and which is used under the same conditions. But there are a number of rivers where spinning is not allowed or is limited to some degree and on these rivers it is at times essential to be able to fish with the deeply sunken fly.

Sunk-line fishing

The first requisite of sunk-line fishing is a line which sinks as deeply in the water as possible. The salmon in his comfortable lie on the river bed is loath to move far in cold conditions and it is essential to present the fly close to him. To handle the sunk line—and modern sinking lines sink quickly and deeply, you need a strong rod. Indeed some rods are still specially made for this comparitively little used method. On the Tweed, for example, where you are limited to 'fly only' at the beginning and end of the season, enormous 'poles' are used to force out the heavy lines and huge leaded flies.

Salmon fishing on the River Spey at Grantown

With a big rod and sunk line, a big fly is usually used and of these the tube fly and the 'Elverine' are, I think, the best. At times, however, particularly in autumn, salmon sometimes take a much smaller sunk fly. It is difficult to define big and small in regard to salmon flies because what is enormous on one river is thought tiny on another, but let me, as a guide, define large as two inches long and small as half an inch long.

Sunk-line fishing mostly consists of casting the longest possible line across and downstream and allowing it to swing round in the current as slowly as possible. Sometimes it is necessary to

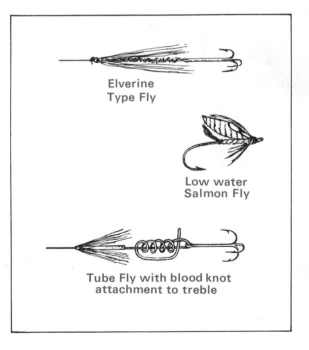

Elverine
Type Fly

Low water
Salmon Fly

Tube Fly with blood knot
attachment to treble

The head of the cock salmon showing the hooked lower jaw or 'kype'

A selection of the home-made wooden Devon Minnows. These lures can be made very cheaply with the minimum of tools, and they catch fish!

cast upstream to make sure the line sinks deeply. A belly of line thrown upstream just after the cast has landed obviously delays the pull of the current through the line to the fly, letting it sink and helping it to move slowly. This is called mending and I will deal with this in more detail when we reach the floating line.

When the line has fished round and is hanging below you, let it remain there for a second or two, then move down two steps and cast again. You will probably find it necessary to pull in a certain amount of line and it is the need to cast and lift a long sunken line which makes this style of fishing much easier to describe than to use. Fish usually take firmly, you feel a strong pull and they hook themselves.

Heavy spinning in winter

Spinning is an easier method of taking fish in cold or high water, although I consider it still more difficult than floating-line fly fishing. Here, certainly on all but small rivers, you need a double-handed rod and a multiplier or fixed spool reel loaded with 12 lb. breaking strain line. In the early part of the season and sometimes at the 'back end' you should seek to fish your bait as slowly as possible. This is because, as I have previously said, in cold water for most of the time the salmon does not move far to take a lure.

There is a vast number of different spinning lures, but for this type of work I now rely entirely on wooden or buoyant Devons. Not so very long ago, in spring fishing, if you were not bumping the bottom with a heavily-leaded bait it was thought you had no chance of a fish. Using a wooden Devon, which can be fished really slowly without becoming caught up on the bottom, it has been found that fish come up a long way to take an unleaded bait. I usually use a small Hillman lead—a bullet with a soft wire link fixed to a ball-bearing swivel, at the top of the yard or so of nylon to which the Devon is attached. This gives a little extra casting weight and prevents any kink through the spinning action of the Devon. It is only on very cold days when fish are dour that I find it necessary to put on more lead and bump the bottom.

Fishing the wooden Devon is a particularly pleasant form of angling, akin to fishing the floating line.

I like to use a ten-foot rod, a multiplier, fifteen-pound white braided Terylene and a yard or so of ten-pound monofilament as a trace. I use a white line because I can see it easily, for it is both useful and exciting to be able to watch your line. Cast across and slightly downstream and if there is an upstream wind, use a high trajectory cast so that an upstream billow is formed in the line. This helps to slow-up the swing of the Devon across the stream.

As soon as the bait drops in the water, apply the reel check. Continue the cast holding the rod as high as possible to keep as much line out of the water as you can to prevent the drag of the current pulling at the Devon. The salmon's take is particularly exciting, often the first indication is a straightening of the line.

The size of bait varies from river to river, but for early fishing 2 to 2½ inches is most suitable. With regard to colour, ring the changes between a yellow belly, black and gold, brown and gold, and blue and silver and you will not go far wrong.

In recommending a braided line when most anglers use monofilament I may sound old-fashioned, but being able to see the line does make a big difference in controlling the bait's speed. If you use a fixed spool reel, of course, you must use monofilament.

Floating-line fishing

As the weather warms up, usually in April, the fly fished with the floating line comes into its own. It is, I think, the most pleasant form of salmon fishing and probably the most effective.

On all but small rivers, or under very low water conditions, the long double-handed rod gives many advantages in line control. The cast should be about the length of the rod, of monofilament somewhere between six and ten pounds breaking strain, according to conditions. The fly should either be a sparsely-dressed fly of the type known as 'low water' in sizes 4 to 10, or a tube fly. The wise angler carries a tin of Fuller's earth or a piece of potter's clay which, if applied to the nylon of the cast, causes it to sink at once.

There are several styles of fishing the floating line and variations on all of them to suit different conditions, of which speed and direction of current are most important. For the benefit of this exercise, however, let us split floating-line fishing into two methods, the 'square' and the 'less square'. Of these, and I have turned full circle in my methods, the latter is the easier.

Floating-line fishing is best practised in water

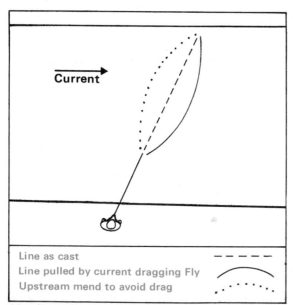

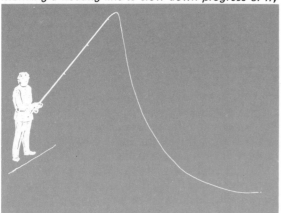

Mending a floating line to slow down progress of fly

Line as cast	– – – –
Line pulled by current dragging Fly	⌒
Upstream mend to avoid drag	··········

Correct angle of rod and line when fishing with floating line. There should be ample slack line between rod top and fly

which is running at a good pace. In late spring, when the water may well be on the cool side, fish avoid lies in very strong water. As the weather warms up they are to be found more and more in rough, broken water and in high summer they lie in the roughest and often the very shallow water, particularly towards dusk.

I like to start fishing at the head of a run, casting a longish line across and downstream. The angle of cast must vary according to the set of the current, but if the beginner casts somewhere between ten and fiteen degrees downstream of an imaginary line across the river, he will not go too far wrong.

As soon as a cast is made and the line falls on the water, make one mend. That is, throw a loop in the middle of your line upstream to steady the speed at which your fly will fish across the current. At the beginner's stage, one mend is enough –indeed the experienced angler rarely needs more. If I can start a novice on a nice 'popple' (a stretch of river where the current runs fairly briskly over shallows causing a rippled surface) I stop him mending completely.

Overmending is a most common fault and is the result of all sorts of nonsense being written about the need to have your fly fishing lifelessly 'like a floating leaf'. Take no notice of such advice. Your fly needs life and this is imparted by the pull of the line. What you must seek to do is to prevent your fly fishing so fast that it ceases to look natural.

Having made your mend, allow the line to swing round in the current holding your rod high with a good slack loop hanging down from the rod top to the point where the line meets the water. When a salmon takes, it usually rises slowly from its lie, takes the fly, holding it lightly, and does not really shut its mouth firmly until it is well on the way back to its resting place. It is normally useless to strike, for this results only in pulling the fly out of the salmon's mouth or in the fish feeling resistance and expelling the hook. With this style of fishing the first indication you have of a take is your line lifting, straightening, and then moving away. It is, for me, the most thrilling moment in fishing.

The right thing to do is nothing. Provided you have a nice slack loop, as described, the salmon feels no resistance until it is well down in the water with its mouth firmly closed. You see your line go, tighten, and then feel the pull of a well hooked fish.

After your fly has fished round to a position below you, leave it there a second or two as a fish often follows the lure. After this brief pause, pull in several feet of line with your left hand. This causes the fly to lift and move upstream and if there is a following fish, it may well take. If not, move down two or three yards and cast again. One of the worst mistakes in salmon fishing is to show the fish a fly or a bait too often. It

A typical spring salmon: big, deep, and heavy. A magnificent fish by any standards

is a sound tactic to fish down a pool leaving good big gaps between each cast, and then fish it down again casting in the gaps.

In the other basic style, you cast a shorter line almost square across the river. Obviously with the direct pull of the current on the middle of the line you need to mend more often and your fly fishes faster and higher up in the water. When fish take they frequently break the surface, often in a very pretty head-and-tail rise and for this reason many anglers prefer this method. I find it difficult not to react like a trout angler and tighten the line when a fish takes like this.

The correct drill in most cases is to have a yard or two of slack line in the left hand which is released as the fish rises. This both gives the fish time to close its mouth and also ensures a good hook-hold. The salmon, through the pull of the line curved in the current, is usually hooked in the 'scissors'–the tough corner of the mouth.

Anglers differ in opinion as to whether the fly should be 'worked'–that is, given extra life by pulling in a foot or so of line at a time. I do not think it essential, but I do usually pull once or twice as my cast fishes round. When fishing for grilse it does pay to move your fly in this way.

There is one other method of fly fishing in the summer that is particularly useful for grilse. In conditions of low water and high temperature fish will, as I have said, lie in fast, shallow, broken water. Here a dropper fly, one tied to a short link about halfway up the cast, allowed to trip along the water surface as the tail fly fishes round, often brings fish to the surface in a thrilling, boiling take.

These are the basic methods of summer fly fishing for salmon. They are both effective, exciting, and relatively easy. Earlier I mentioned that I considered spinning more difficult. This is because with spinning tackle it is not easy to continue casting exactly the same length of line and thus cover every inch of the pool. With a fly rod, once you have made one cast of, let us say, 18 yards, every decent cast thereafter will be of that length.

The choice of fly can be complicated, for there is a vast number of different patterns which has been built up over many years. I find I use few patterns but in three or four different sizes. With Blue Charm, Logie, Thunder and Lightning, and a black pattern such as a Black Heron, I am quite happy.

As the angler is seeking to imitate something in nature and make it look right and behave right from the salmon's point of view, colour and size are important. By and large, the warmer the water, the smaller the fly. In rough conditions you usually need a bigger fly than in smooth water. When fishing a glide, such as the tail of a pool, a double-hooked fly will help to pierce the solid body of water. 'Bright day, bright fly; dull day, dull fly', is a sound basis for choice and if the sun is shining into the salmon's eyes, a black fly is the best bet.

Summer spinning

There are several methods of spinning used in the warmer months and for the most part these demand light tackle and the fixed spool reel. The warmer the weather and the lower the river level, the smaller the bait should be, and salmon sometimes will take only half-inch Devons and similar small baits.

In summer the bait can be fished fairly quickly and indeed one of the most successful methods of catching salmon is to throw a small Devon upstream over the fish and wind it downstream as fast as possible. Why salmon take a Devon or small spoon fished in this manner is one of the many mysteries of the sport, but take it that they do, usually with a bang and more often than not they are hooked right back in the mouth.

When the water is coloured in a spate, salmon can be caught on spinning tackle and for this method I prefer the double-handed rod and the multiplier. Salmon can be hard to handle in strong current and a long, powerful rod is a help.

The lure *par excellence* in a spate, is a spoon. Most patterns work well but my favourite is either black and gold or orange and black. Both these show up well even in coloured water.

When salmon are running they swim high in the water and I have had best results spinning close to the top with the bait being retrieved quickly.

Natural baits

These then are the normal methods of fishing for salmon. They are also caught on natural baits. A sprat, gold or silver, mounted on special tackle used to be a very popular bait and is still well

The rod arches as a salmon is drawn towards the gaff at the conclusion of an exciting fight

worth a trial. The prawn, usually boiled and preserved and fished on a single hook, 'sink and draw' or on a mount with fins which makes it spin is widely used. I hate the prawn because frequently it disturbs and frightens fish and I think we would all be better off if its use were banned, as it is on some rivers.

Finally there is the humble worm. There is a great deal in worming for salmon and because I have done little of it I have asked one or two experts how they set about it. They agree that the worm should be fished so that it trundles along the bottom and that it should be allowed to come to rest just on the edge of the current. The salmon follows it into the slack and takes it there.

Playing and landing a salmon

Having hooked your salmon, what do you do then? Let us first look at how you play and land salmon with a fly outfit.

Unlike sea trout and other fish, which go off like a bomb when hooked, the salmon usually does little for several seconds or longer. This gives you time to wind in any slack line, and, if wading, to move to dry ground or to shallow water where you can wade easily. In playing a fish you have a number of weapons. You have the spring of the rod which absorbs the pull of the fish. You have the reel which allows the fish to take line and allows you to retrieve it. You have a number of tactics which are both easily explained and easily practised.

The first and most important rule is to keep a steady tight line the whole time. This is best done by holding the rod with the butt pointing at about 60 degrees, at which angle it is both putting a tiring strain on the fish and using its spring to the full to absorb strain. If the fish swims away from you, let it go by allowing the reel to give line. When playing a fish try to keep more or less opposite to it and if it runs downstream, follow it if you can. If there is a high bank behind you it pays to stand on it, because in this way more line can be kept out of the water. If a strong fish like a salmon jumps or pulls heavily against a long curved line in the water, it can break the cast or shed the hook. If a salmon jumps, or plunges on the surface, drop the rod point slightly to give slack line.

There are two important tactics which can be used when playing any fish. The first is side

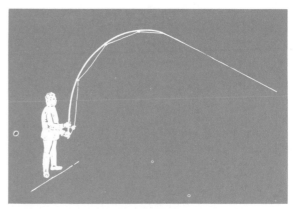

Rod held too high and too far from body

strain. If the rod is canted over from the near vertical to the near horizontal the fish can be forced to swim round in the direction of the strain. In this way the hooked fish can be guided away from obstacles it might be able to use to foul the line. The other is known as 'walking up'. Let us suppose your salmon has managed to swim well below you and that you are prevented in some way from following downstream to take up a position opposite the fish. It is therefore important to bring the fish upstream. This is as easy to perform as it is to describe.

You place one hand on the reel to prevent it revolving. Then keeping the rod reasonably high, you walk upstream and the fish follows you like a dog on a lead.

It is important to ensure that the reel does not give line. If it does, the check vibration may frighten the salmon and make it run. When you have walked up a fish or two, you will become quite blasé about what at first seemed a difficult operation and move your fish by holding the rod over your shoulder and walking upstream without even a backward glance.

A fish should be played until it is tired out. This is the crucial moment in the struggle, for the sudden plunge on a short line has allowed many a fish to escape. If possible keep out of sight as long as possible – it is the sight of you which gives the salmon the extra strength to make that last plunge.

There are three main methods of landing salmon. A big net is becoming ever more popular, as you can land the fish in an awkward place without marking it. The net should be well sunk, and the fish drawn over it before lifting. I do not like gaffing fish but there are occasions when it is

the only possible way of landing them. Try to present the fish either to yourself, or to whoever is gaffing for you, so that it is broadside on. Place the gaff carefully across the salmon's back slightly ahead of the dorsal fin and with a smooth firm stroke pull in the gaff and lift out the fish.

The best method of all is beaching. Where you have a shallow beach, play out your fish until it is on its side. If you keep firm gentle pressure on the salmon it wriggles partially onto the beach. Maintain gentle pressure, walk round behind the fish, take it by the tail and either push it up onto the beach, or lift it onto dry ground. The first action after a fish is landed should be to despatch it with a smart blow on the head.

Playing a fish on spinning tackle is basically similar. The main difference is that both the multiplier and the fixed spool reels are highly geared and while with a fly reel you can 'winch' your fish towards you, with the other two you have to recover line by what is called 'pumping'. This action consists of lowering the rod point towards the fish, at the same time winding to recover line. The reel is then prevented from turning by, in the case of the multiplier, thumb-pressure, and in the case of the fixed spool reel, finger-pressure, and the rod is lifted into the vertical. This pulls the fish towards the angler and allows line to be recovered. Although pumping is generally looked upon as a technique for use with spinning reels it is sound practice with

An angler admires the clean lines of a handsome spring salmon from the River Severn

a fly outfit.

With both fly reel and multiplier it is often desirable to apply pressure to the reel drum with either finger or thumb when a fish is running. This is a different problem with the fixed spool reel, for here line is given to a running fish through the slipping clutch and recovered by the rotation of the pick up.

Many good anglers set their slipping clutches on the light side and apply extra pressure by pressing the forefinger against the spool lip. The action of the slipping clutch in giving line, and the pick up during recovery does put twist in the line and this, over the period of a hard fight with a salmon, can weaken the line seriously. There is one reel, however, the Intrepid 'Elite', which has an ingenious mechanism which allows the handle to revolve backwards, if desired, against a check, like a fly or multiplying reel. I find a reel of this type both more pleasant to use and more efficient. On all fixed spool reels there is an anti-reverse mechanism which when engaged prevents the handle turning back. This can be useful when landing a fish.

One final point. Having landed your fish you may have to carry it some distance. A straw bass or a salmon carrier makes the whole operation much more comfortable.

Dave Burr

Match Fishing Tactics

Before discussing the various tackle set-ups used on different waters, there are several terms that must be understood.

. First of all the sizes and importance of split shot must be mastered. Even the novice knows split shot have but one function—to cock the float. With more experience the angler learns the importance of where on the line to use the shot for different conditions and what sizes to use. Size and position of the shot will determine the nature of bite indication given by the float. It will also present the bait correctly but when positioned incorrectly it can be a reason for failure. Throughout this chapter positions of shot will be suggested, but these can only be a guide. Each time the angler ventures out, different conditions prevail and conventional methods will often give way to the unorthodox.

Shot have a rather confusing set of numbers and letters to define their respective sizes. The largest are called SSG, or more commonly, swan shot. Next size is AAA, then BB. Numbers take over as the shot get smaller, with a series of one to eight—eight being the smallest. Each is just a little smaller than its predecessor, so that with a full range the float can be weighted down to within very fine margins.

It must be remembered that the nearer the shot to the hook, the sharper the bite. Fish will feel the weight, however slight and if their suspicions are roused often drop the bait. Shot too far away from the hook enables the fish to sample the bait with no indication on the float. Still waters require methods of shotting that are different to running waters.

Floats are perhaps the most fascinating part of coarse fishing. Basically we have to consider two types. Light floats are used on canals, small slow moving rivers and any other small waters where casting distance is of little concern. These floats are also ideal for use when after small fry near the banks of larger rivers.

The heavier floats are for big waters, like the Thames, Severn, Welland, Huntspill, Witham, etc. Here floats are needed that will carry a fair amount of weight, ride a powerful current, or by virtue of their shape enable the angler to master bad conditions.

I have illustrated a number of floats, which though not a complete list would rarely leave anyone beaten. Within this range there is a float for all occasions.

There are various materials from which they can be made. Stems can be made of quill or cane and some stick-type floats use wire which makes them almost self cocking. Cane is a good material, not very buoyant and therefore ideal for the antennae of sliding floats. A heavy material, it also helps to add distance when casting. Quill is also a first-class material and my own personal favourite; the 'ducker' range has a quill stem. Although not easy to shot the inverted quills make very sensitive tips for floats and it will be noted that I have listed two of this type, one for very light fishing and the other with the addition of a cork body to give a heavier shotting pattern. Bodies are usually made from balsa or cork. Both are satisfactory, but balsa is easier to work and gives a better finish.

One type of float that has always been popular

(Opposite) It is on such canals as this that the fine-tackle expert often wins the day

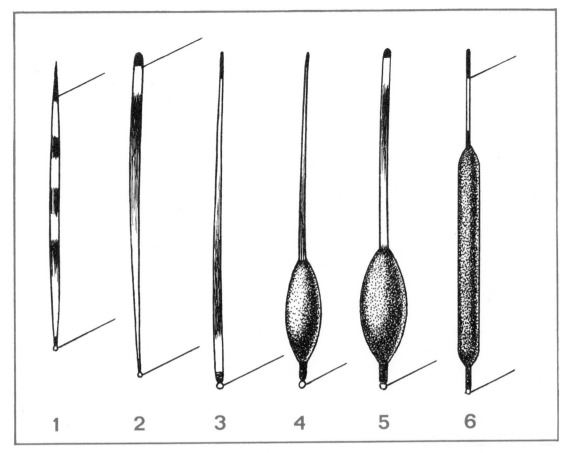

Floats for canals and very slow-moving waters

1. Small porcupine quill for general use 2. Crow quill for slow shallow streams 3. Inverted crow quill for canals 4. Onion type—cork on quill: for choppy days; extra shot needed for casting 5. The famous 'Midland ducker'—cork on quill: all-round float for light fishing 6. A slim float for canals and streams fished top and bottom or bottom only, ideal for caster fishing

(Above) Where one perch is caught there is usually a shoal that could make up a match-winning catch

(Opposite) The 1968 European freshwater fishing championship held on the River Blackwater in Ireland

(Right) Coloured baits can often mean the difference between success and failure

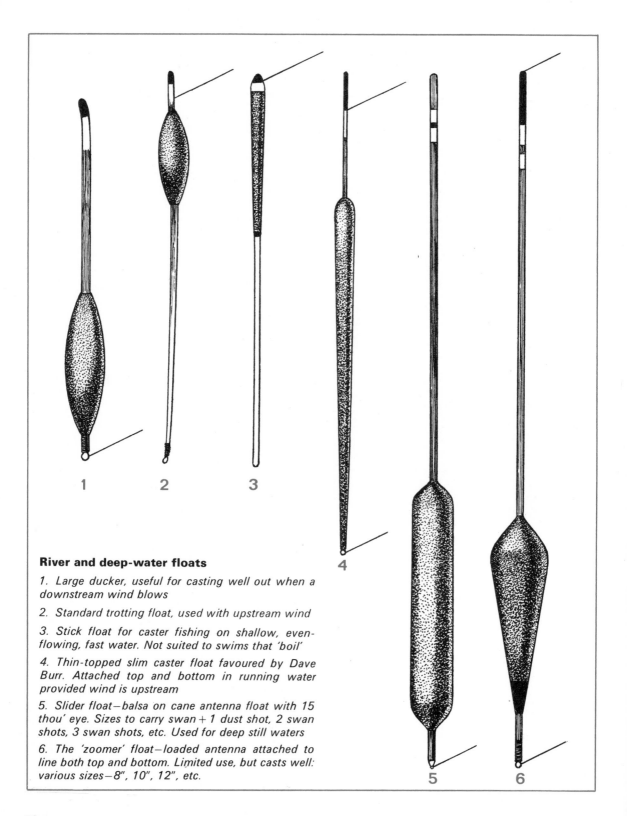

River and deep-water floats

1. Large ducker, useful for casting well out when a downstream wind blows

2. Standard trotting float, used with upstream wind

3. Stick float for caster fishing on shallow, even-flowing, fast water. Not suited to swims that 'boil'

4. Thin-topped slim caster float favoured by Dave Burr. Attached top and bottom in running water provided wind is upstream

5. Slider float—balsa on cane antenna float with 15 thou' eye. Sizes to carry swan + 1 dust shot, 2 swan shots, 3 swan shots, etc. Used for deep still waters

6. The 'zoomer' float—loaded antenna attached to line both top and bottom. Limited use, but casts well: various sizes—8", 10", 12", etc.

is the porcupine quill. It has a good shape, but personally I have never been happy with it when casting. For under the rod tip fishing, however, it has few equals and that is why there are a few small ones in my tackle box.

Peacock quill is another ideal material for float making. Extremely light, it can be used in short lengths for canal fishing or in longer lengths for larger waters. For long-distance fishing a long peacock quill with a balsa body set well down and loaded with lead, enables great accuracy to be coupled with fine sensitivity. The light stem with the lead loaded end make this float like a dart and that is the name it has been given. Waters like the Great Ouse Relief Channel, with an 85 yd. width, can be fished mid-stream quite easily with the dart.

I now intend to take each type of water, dis-

Features such as the milk factory on this canal, often mark the best swims in the vicinity because of the abundance of food that finds its way into the water

cussing terminal tackle, ways of fishing, baiting, hooks sizes and line strengths.

Canals and small still waters

The matchman almost always sets out to catch roach, unless he has prior knowledge about a bream swim. Here 1½ lb. b.s. line is adequate and a start should be made with a size 18 or 20 fine wire hook. Roach may be feeding in mid-water, so the nearest shot should be at about 18 in. from the hook—a No. 8 dust shot. Assuming a depth of 4 ft. only one other shot will be required and there is no need for this to be larger than a No. 1. Any additional lead required can be placed on the float itself in the form of lead wire, or shot can be placed directly under the float. The float must be attached at the bottom only, so that any surface movement can be defeated by sinking the line. Line sinking can be done by submerging the rod tip and making one or two turns of the reel to take up the slack.

Although catches of fish are sometimes made quite close to the near bank, activity before a match invariably sends the fish over to the far bank. This is most apparent in the summer months. On a wide canal it is not possible to feed with loose maggots alone and groundbait must also be used. This should be kept to a minimum although regular offerings are essential. Above all, heavy splashes must be avoided and this applies not only to the groundbait but also to the terminal tackle when cast out.

A canal does not have an even depth and if subject to a certain amount of boat traffic it almost certainly has a boat run. It will be in the deepest part and consequently much of the food upon which the fish feed is pushed onto the shelf at the sides. When long casting this change in depth must be taken into consideration. If there is only 18 in. of water where the terminal tackle lands, any drift on the water will move the bait into the deeper water. Variations of depth must be noted when plumbing. If there is no natural movement it pays to create this by reeling in some line. As the bait comes off the shelf into the deeper water it is often taken by the fish.

A point here about taking the depth. Large plummets are ideal for rivers, but on a canal the addition of a swan shot just above the hook will serve the same purpose without disturbing the water by casting a large piece of lead into the swim.

Bearing in mind there may be a productive feeding area close to the bank, another swim can be fed. As the match progresses and the effects of initial disturbances forgotten, the fish will become confident. If the distant swim becomes non-productive, the second swim gives the angler another chance. In a high wind the closer swim has to be used anyway. Long casting with heavy tackle reduces the chances of catching fish near the bank with light tackle at a later stage in the match.

Terminal tackle arrangement for canals

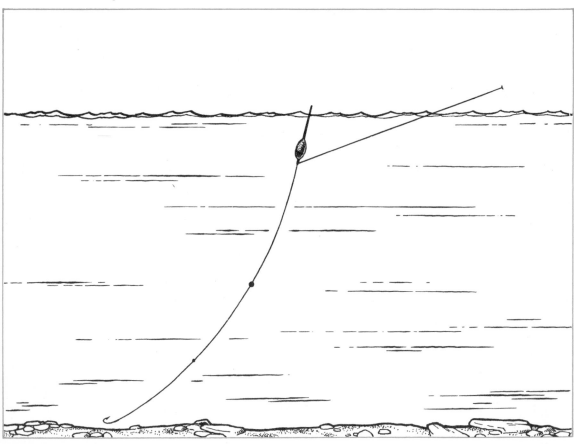

Typical cross-section of canal with boat run. Food will be washed up onto shelves by passing boats

Most canals are at their most productive during the first hour of the match and every effort must be made to take as many fish as possible. Later bites may become less frequent. When the lull starts, scale down the size of the hook, going smaller until bites start again. Baits too will have to be reduced in size.

In the winter fish are more often found in deeper water, even in the boat run itself. A larger bait is generally more successful although for roach, hook size 18 with a suitably sized bait is large enough. If bream are known to be present the approach can be different both with feeding and with the hook-bait. Often bread flake takes the better fish, but do not waste too much time for they are uncertain feeders and small roach more often than not, make up the matchman's canal catches.

On clear-water canals the bread punch is very successful. The tackle set up should be the same as for maggot fishing, with emphasis on lightness, and a slow sinking bait.

The slow river

Here the angler faces natural movement and varying depths. More thought has to be given to feeding, for even with a light flow the bait travels downstream before reaching the bottom.

The light tackle used on canals will not take bait down quickly enough so shotting techniques must be varied. Provided the depth is not too great the floats used on the canal can also be used on the slow river, but the lead used on the canal to load the float is now needed on the line.

A look at the illustration will show the shot grouped well down the line towards the hook. This is done to sink the bait down quickly so that it can be worked around the bottom of the river. It is here the angler can expect to find fish, especially if he is after quality rather than quantity. This tackle can also be used for fish feeding off the bottom. Shots are placed about 3 ft. from the hook, leaving only a small dust shot at 18 in. from the hook. This gives a slow drop and can be adjusted according to the speed of the bites.

Once the depth of the feeding fish has been determined, shot must be strung out to give the bait a steady drop. In the feeding area in the summer, fish accept a moving bait quite readily, but in winter a static bait brings better results. Colder water makes fish lethargic and less inclined to move around looking for food.

Although slightly heavier tackle is required for the slow river than that used on the canal, it must not be too heavy. Great care must be taken in the way it is presented. Bulky shot, placed too near the hook, are not necessary. Fine lines are a must unless good-sized bream are likely to be found. I will now take the reader through a typical match fished on the waters of the Great Ouse—one where bream are likely to be found.

First note the flow of the river and direction of the wind. It may appear deep at the side and this is a good indication that there is a reasonable overall depth of water. The river is about 30 yd. wide so fishing on the far side is not out of the question. However, if there are fish on the near side they will be easier to catch, so that is the place to start.

A float taking about 3 BB shot is selected and as the wind is blowing downstream it is an antenna float, a medium sized 'ducker', that is chosen. Line should be attached to the bottom

Terminal tackle arrangement for slow river with up-stream wind

only so that it can be sunk and remain unaffected by the wind. Depth is estimated at 8 ft. and the 3 BB shot are grouped about 3 ft. from the hook. An additional dust shot is placed 12 in. from the hook. The hook is size 18 crystal tied to $1\frac{1}{2}$ lb. line.

At the whistle begin to plumb the depths. Not in one spot, but several, covering the area which will be fished. In this way likely feeding places can be spotted from the start of the match. I will assume the angler finds that a gradual slope out for five yards to a depth of ten feet has a tendency to slope up towards the end of the swim. This means that if the float is set at 10 ft. it will drag as it goes down the swim. This problem can be overcome by holding back slightly on the float and so raise the bait to a level that will allow it to swim down. Once the right depth is found,

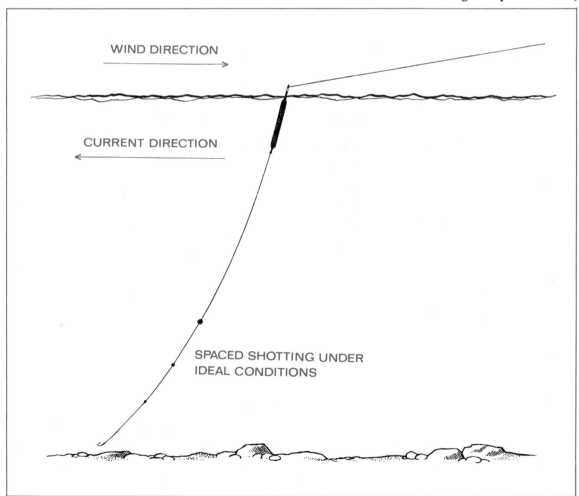

WIND DIRECTION

CURRENT DIRECTION

SPACED SHOTTING UNDER
IDEAL CONDITIONS

one dust shot just under the float gives an indication in case of float slip.

Deciding to fish at the five yard point the angler now introduces groundbait. This should be of the fine variety, but mixed fairly stiffly to allow it to carry the feed put inside. Taking into account the flow, it must be introduced at the head of the swim. The float tackle is cast out immediately to follow the groundbait. If there is any doubt about weed in the swim it will pay to have a trial swim down before putting in any groundbait. The competitor is then sure he has a swim with a good clean bottom. The hook bait first used is a normal large white or special maggot.

Terminal tackle arrangement for slow river with downstream wind

As soon as the end of the swim is reached the float is held back to swing the bait into the bank. The bait will then lie on the bottom and if a bite occurs it indicates that the fish will accept a still bait. If nothing happens, retrieve quietly and quickly. Before recasting to the head of the swim, a ball of groundbait about the size of an egg is thrown into the same place as before. It may be some time before fish are caught, but the same ritual must be followed each swim down.

Let us assume that small roach have been coming regularly, but after a couple of hours bites cease. The fish may have stopped feeding, or perhaps the shoal was small and has been depleted. A pike may have moved in or, most likely, the shoal has moved away from the bank. The angler must now explore further out. Again the plummet is used to determine extra depth.

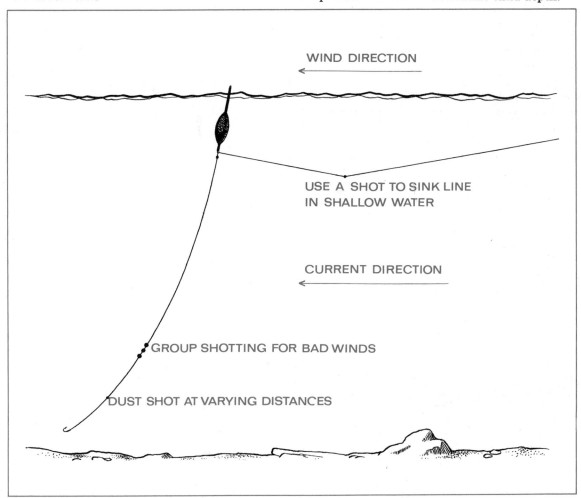

WIND DIRECTION

USE A SHOT TO SINK LINE
IN SHALLOW WATER

CURRENT DIRECTION

GROUP SHOTTING FOR BAD WINDS

DUST SHOT AT VARYING DISTANCES

The weigh-in of the 1968 National Championship held in Norfolk. Here a catch of bream from the River Bure is emptied into the scale pan

The same groundbaiting technique is used—one ball for every swim down—and provided the extra distance can still be attained with ease, there is no need for a change of float. Once fish have been contacted stay with the shoal. If fish cease to feed again go further out into the river, changing to a heavier float if necessary. In this way the whole area is covered.

If it is known that bream shoals inhabit the stretch of water, tactics must be different. Groundbaiting will be done on a larger scale than for roach and the middle of the river is more likely to produce fish than the sides. Being bottom feeders bream prefer the bait to be either still or moving slowly. If the flow is slight the bait can be presented in the following slow method. The shot are bunched at 2 ft. from the hook and the float pushed up so that it is at least a foot over depth. A cast is made well over the middle and downstream. If the wind is upstream the float can be attached top and bottom for better control, but if it is downstream it will be attached at the bottom only. Instead of allowing the tackle to move downstream hold back the float and allow the bait to swing round in an arc. By placing groundbait in a line towards the bank starting at the head of the swim the hookbait should travel throughout the groundbaited area. Here again regular feeding brings the shoal into the swim, and until that happens there is a good chance that roach might still be caught.

A double maggot on a size 16 hook often tempts bream and this is the size of bait to use at the beginning. If nothing happens then try a single maggot on an 18 hook or put on a larger hook and try a bunch of maggots. Bread too is a very good bait for bream and fished in this manner it can be deadly.

Bait quantities are always a problem, but as a rough guide I would suggest the following: half a pint of hook maggots, four pints of feeders and at least 10 lb. of dry groundbait. Some groundbait should be made ready before arriving at the waterside.

If the water being fished is noted for its roach, groundbait will not be needed in large quantities. Indeed, it is sometimes better forgotten unless difficulty is experienced in placing feed in the right spot.

In winter one bait stands out above all others for roach and that is the caster. Better fished close in because of the sharpness of bites, the tackle must be light and small shot should be strung up the line. Roach are prone to come up to the caster and if the shot are spread bites can be detected at any level. Big roach will be taken laying-on with the caster, but as the matchman is often concerned more with quantity than quality, it is best fished on the swim. There is more about caster fishing in the section on fast waters.

The bream waters of fenland

Often called the home of match fishing, the waters in and around the Fen district of East Anglia draw thousands of matchman every week. Wide waters, with little flow, they have always presented special problems and the ingenuity of the match fraternity has been taxed to the full.

The wide drains like the Welland, the North Bank, the Great Ouse Relief Channel and the Witham, are really rivers, but man has control over them and this means that in all but floodtimes the angler does not have much flow to consider. The Witham behaves most like a river, but there will be days even on the Witham with no visible flow.

In the flat surrounding country in which these waters are found, the slightest breeze can seem like a gale. The bream that abound in these waters are the match winners and must be sought unless team tactics decide otherwise. Unfortunately bream are rarely within easy casting distance and long casts to the far bank will often have to be made. Imagine the problems. Long casts, deep water in most waters except the Welland, windy conditions on most occasions and timid bites from fish that are perhaps the most educated in the land.

A few years ago the man who was master of float fishing invariably won the day. Nowadays he has been overhauled by the men who use the leger as an aid to long casting.

Float fishing is the more difficult method to use at a distance and I will deal with this technique first.

Antennae floats must be used, for drift created by the wind will move the surface water quite quickly and a still bait must be presented. Long distance casting is required and tackle must be heavy, carrying in the region of two or three swan shot. This will depend on the strength of the wind and its direction and if it blows really strongly, floats carrying even four or five swan shot will become necessary.

The rod most generally used will be of 13 ft. length. Some anglers use a 12 ft. rod but this is a matter of choice. Line strengths of 2½–3 lb. will be adequate and naturally, a fixed spool reel is the only reel worth using.

For deep water a sliding float is used. There are some who use the 'zoomer' (see float illustrations) and this is fixed to the line at whatever depth is encountered. Casting into 14 or 15 ft. of water, the zoomer is not always suitable because of bankside vegetation. For this reason the slider is a far better proposition.

The modern slider is a far cry from those produced a few years ago. It incorporates only one very small eye, of a diameter hardly bigger than that of the line that passes through it. The stop that is used can be very small. For this a piece of nylon that is only slightly larger in diameter than the reel line, is used. It will be able to slide up and down the line so that depth adjustments can be made with ease. The method of tying this special knot is shown in the diagram. You will note that the ends are not cut, but left long— about 2 in. It will enable the knot to travel through the rod rings without impeding the cast. Variations of this float for deep moving water are described later.

The main advantage of the slider is that it helps easy casting, for the float rests on the highest shot and as this is normally only a short distance from the hook there is no chance of the float tangling round the top of the rod. Another important feature is the directness of strike. The line passes through the float ring and the strike is made direct to the fish. This enables the angler to respond quickly to a bite without the loss of impetus caused by hitting a heavy float fixed to the line.

The importance of sinking the line cannot be stressed too much. On all waters wind will move the surface and if the line is allowed to remain on the surface it will bow. This reduces the effectiveness of the strike as well as causing a delay sufficient to give the fish time to drop the bait. The line is sunk by overcasting, then as soon as the float has righted the rod top is placed well under the water. A few turns of the handle of the reel will sink the line as well as straightening it. Once the line is sunk the rod is raised until it is just above the surface.

Group shotting is recommended as this will

Regardless of technique or venue, the angler who keeps away from the water's edge and makes the least possible disturbance, will catch more fish

reduce tangles. Many bites are of the lift variety, caused by the fish raising the lowest shot. In rough weather this shot should be large, so that adequate indication of the lift is given. Remember, it must not be too near the hook as this gives very sharp bites that are difficult to connect with at long distances. There are exceptions to most rules and in this case the shot may have to be put close to the hook if the fish bite timidly and the strike should be made as soon as possible.

Casting a plummet long distances is not easy, so for depth-finding a swan shot is added to the hook length. This is in addition to the capacity of the float and by increasing the depth by 6 in. each time it is obvious when the swan shot has reached the bottom. Make a mental note of the position of the nylon stop so that in the event of an adjustment, a quick return to the original position can be made if necessary.

Groundbaiting techniques are the same whatever method is chosen and this also applies to hooks and baits. I will now deal with legering methods.

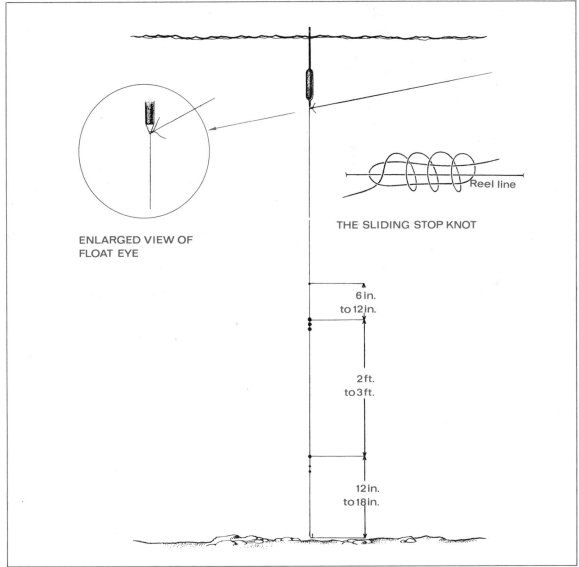

ENLARGED VIEW OF
FLOAT EYE

THE SLIDING STOP KNOT

Reel line

6 in.
to 12 in.

2 ft.
to 3 ft.

12 in.
to 18 in.

Sliding float tackle arrangement for deep slow-moving or still waters

Legering principles of the specimen hunter have been adopted by the matchman, but with a difference in the method of bite detection. Long association with float fishing has prompted the matchman to use indicators that react in a similar way. One of these indicators and by far the most widely used, is the swing tip. Originally devised by a Boston man – Jack Clayton – it has been modified, although the principle has remained the same.

Attached to the end of the rod, it is free to swing. The line runs through rings on the tip and the resultant pull from a fish moves it up in an arc. Being flexible it has no effect on the way a fish is played and presents no handicap in casting. With a quarter or half ounce lead and a steady swing long casts can be achieved with ease. Practice soon enables the angler to place his bait accurately.

There are many variations of the terminal tackle used in legering, but the one illustrated has been found to be the most effective. This is particularly so on well-fished waters where the

85

(Above) Catches on the wide rivers will often include large numbers of bream thus making big keepnets a necessity

(Below) A bowl is used for mixing up large quantities of groundbait, its consistency will depend on the type of water being fished

slightest amount of resistance causes fish to drop the bait. This is the reason why a split ring is used as a stop in addition to the split ring used on the running link.

The position of the stop depends on conditions and feeding habits of the fish. For still water it can be as much as 3 ft. away but in running water it should be a little closer. If it is found that the bait is being taken on the 'drop', the stop can be moved further away from the hook, giving the long tail plenty of time to reach bottom. A further refinement is the attachment to the nylon link of a float that almost supports the lead. This makes the bait drop slowly.

As I mentioned in the chapter on tackle, the rod for legering should be about 10 ft. long. It should not be used directly in front of the angler but almost parallel with the bank. Bites can be detected easily and the bank gives some protection from the wind. A flat strike should be made.

If wind affects the tip, a windshield should be used. This also serves as a means of detecting bites and some anglers have named this device the target board. There are several varieties and the best are made from heavy gauge perspex. The clear perspex is alternated with black patches and the slightest movement of the tip can be detected as it moves from black portions to clear.

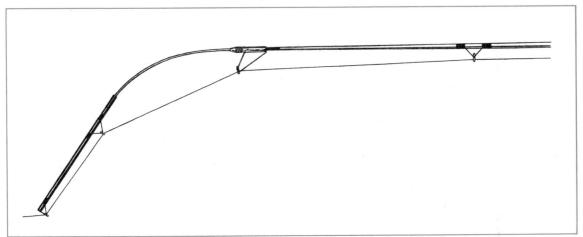

Typical swing tip with screw attachment for fitting to specially adapted tip tings now found on many rods. The flexible section is made of nylon

The link leger using light-weight stops

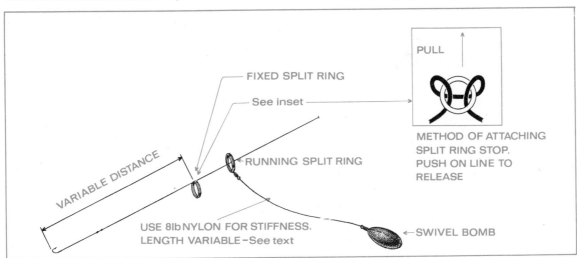

FIXED SPLIT RING

See inset

PULL

METHOD OF ATTACHING SPLIT RING STOP. PUSH ON LINE TO RELEASE

VARIABLE DISTANCE

RUNNING SPLIT RING

USE 8lb NYLON FOR STIFFNESS. LENGTH VARIABLE – See text

SWIVEL BOMB

Position of rod and target board when swing-tip fishing

For closer work a quarter-ounce bomb is heavy enough and on small waters or where a slow dropping bait is required, swan shot can be placed on the nylon link. They are added until the required distance is achieved. The length of the link can have an effect on bites, but is largely dependent on the nature of the bottom. Where silkweed is present it should be fairly long, about 10 in., for this will prevent the bait being buried in the weed. On a hard gravelly bottom the link can be as short as 3 in.

Being concerned with large drains and with bream in mind, groundbaiting is very important. Fairly large quantities are required, although not as much as many would have us believe. The most important point about groundbaiting at long range is accuracy. When float fishing the position of the hookbait is fairly obvious but when legering there is no visible indication of the whereabouts of the bait. Great concentration must be maintained so that each cast is performed with the same effort. This also applies to groundbaiting. Often there is a shadow feature, created by the opposite bank, a tree, bush or telegraph pole. This gives the angler something to aim at, but on wide wind-swept waters such features are seldom present.

Helpful points for greater accuracy are (1) always use a leger weight heavy enough for easy casting. Once a forced cast is made accuracy suffers. (2) Keep the size of each groundbait ball consistent. Very large balls are not recommended because of heavy splash. Small amounts are difficult to throw accurately. (3) The way the groundbait is mixed determines whether long distances can be achieved, especially as there are feeder maggots included in the bait. Either too wet or too dry and the groundbait does not bind. Do not forget to add demarara sugar. It helps binding yet allows the bait to retain the qualities which make it break up easily. If the drain has a good flow the bait should be mixed to bind well, so the breaking up process occurs when the bait is well down in the water. Otherwise the angler feeds the swim belonging to the man downstream.

A great deal is heard about anglers who use enormous amounts of groundbait when bream

There is no standard size for the windshield or target, but it should correspond with the length of tip being used. A good stake is fitted and the board stuck into the bankside.

The butt indicator is also popular, mainly because it can be easily attached to the normal match rod. This is also a free-swinging device, not affected by the wind as it moves in only one plane. Tackle shops carry a wide variety of indicators and some can be fitted further up the rod if desired. They are a refinement of the ball of paste or 'dough bobbin' method still favoured by many specimen hunters. Some of these indicators employ a protractor type gauge to show the slightest bite and on hard-finished waters these are extremely useful.

Use of weight on the terminal tackle depends on the distance being cast and the flow of the water. For the accuracy which is so essential and a quick drop to the groundbaited swim, a half-ounce Arlesey bomb is recommended, especially if the far bank of a wide water is being fished.

The Fens are not the only place for match-winning bream as this happy angler shows with a 26 lb. catch from the River Severn

fishing. These tactics may be used when it is known that a large bream shoal is present, but it is seldom known for sure.

Far better to introduce smaller quantities in a regular fashion knowing that if no bream are present, there is still a chance that roach are feeding. Heavy baiting almost certainly puts roach off the feed and if there are no bream, the chances of a win in the match are slim. There are some who believe the best way is to put in a large quantity of groundbait at the start and then feed lightly. On some waters this is a good idea; especially on the Welland where the shallow water does not lend itself to consistently heavy baiting. Other anglers have enjoyed good results by feeding small particles continuously. Personally I prefer the continuous introduction of smaller particles, believing the heavy introduction of bait is rather hit and miss.

Groundbaiting on any scale is used to take out feeders and for Fenland bream one feeder stands out above all others. This is the squat. Although I do not advocate large quantities of groundbait for this type of fishing, the same cannot be said for my views on feeders. For a big water in an open match, at least a gallon of squats is required. For a smaller match it is possible to get away with smaller quantities, but when bream fishing in Fenland I would never take less than half a gallon. It is surprisingly easy to dispose of such an amount when used in conjunction with groundbait. Bream are gluttonous fish and need plenty of feed to keep them occupied for any length of time.

On the small drains, which provide excellent fishing, there are plenty of bream and generally they tend to be bigger than those of the rivers. Tackle rigs suggested for canals should prove adequate. Winter brings more flow and less weed and during these months drains should be fished in the same way as slow rivers.

When wind problems arise legering usually supplies the answer. In the summer the roach and rudd provide good sport. The usual summer pattern is that bream feed during the first part of the match and later in the day, when bream cease to feed, roach and rudd provide the rest of the catch. A slowly-dropping bait under a small float usually brings roach and rudd to the net, often with a few really good specimens. Many baits succeed on these waters and bread, the most popular, is probably the best for bream.

For roach and rudd a gozzer, anatto, yellow or pinkie are the best maggot baits.

The fast waters

One of the best known of the faster waters is the Trent. Although my comments are based on knowledge gained from fishing this river the same ideas are applicable to similar waters.

Unless a really heavy flow is encountered a large float is not necessary. Size of the float is governed by the depth of water. If there is only about three feet of water a float carrying three small shot will suffice. Four feet requires four small shot and so on up to 10 ft. when depth and pull of water present different problems. Shot should be of size three or four and in a gentle flow size five is adequate.

The shot should be spaced out down the line. In a fairly strong flow bite indication occurs most satisfactorily if the bait preceeds the float downstream. Bites are sharp for the strung-out shot keeps the line straight and any activity is registered immediately on the float. If the shot is bunched direct contact is lost, because the line is bowed and bites are registered less quickly.

The illustration shows the line coming from the top of the float and this is a must for all fast stream fishing. The only time the line is attached to the bottom ring only is when a bad downstream wind occurs.

In shallow water fish take the bait at varying depths. Loose feed is swirled about in the current and the hookbait must behave in the same way. This is another reason for light tackle. The current can take the bait where it will, but if the line is loaded, the bait behaves in an unnatural manner.

Groundbait is only necessary when long distance fishing. Feeding is the most important part—as it is with all match fishing—and in the fast stream it must be constant. What is missed by the fish is quickly carried away by the current and only a really hungry shoal chases downstream for it. More often than not, fish gather at the source of the feed.

This is where the experienced match angler can draw fish away from his downstream rivals. By feeding down to the next man he can induce fish to move up into his own swim. Once he has established his shoal he must be careful not to bring them too far for the angler immediately above him could then use the same tactics.

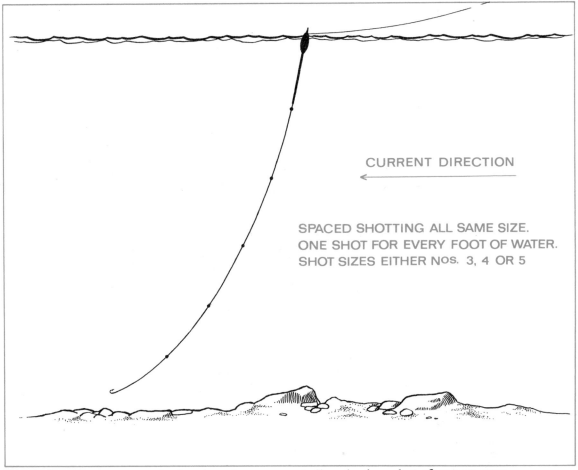

CURRENT DIRECTION

SPACED SHOTTING ALL SAME SIZE.
ONE SHOT FOR EVERY FOOT OF WATER.
SHOT SIZES EITHER NOS. 3, 4 OR 5

Terminal tackle arrangement for fast deep rivers

The term 'constant feeding' confuses many anglers. It is not possible to introduce a constant supply of feed into the swim, but a few feeders every swim down must be the rule.

This is where the hard work begins. If groundbait is used, the same system must apply.

For work close to the bank, a porcupine quill float is ideal, but when the wind is blowing away from the angler or upstream, the 'stick' float is probably best. Bouyant at the top, it was designed for this type of fishing.

A crow quill is also useful, though the addition of a barrel cork near the top makes it more stable. In a downstream wind, control is difficult and in these conditions an antenna-type float attached only to the bottom ring is the best to use. If fishing is still difficult, the line has to be continually lifted and put back behind the float–a tedious business but often necessary.

Tiny hooks are not recommended unless drastic measures force their use. Bites are normally sharp and a larger hook stands more chance of finding a hold. Sizes 18 and 16 serve most purposes with a 20 as a last resort.

Most of this advice is given assuming that roach and dace are the quarry. Chub are an entirely different matter. They are a more cautious fish and will rarely be found close to the bank. If chub are the quarry light tackle should be sacrificed for more substantial floats, which can easily ride the current down the middle of the river.

Returning to roach, one of the most delightful ways of taking quality fish is by using casters.

The light tackle already discussed for fast water fishing is ideal when using casters. A size 16 hook is recommended, with an 18 as a standby, and no groundbait should be used in water

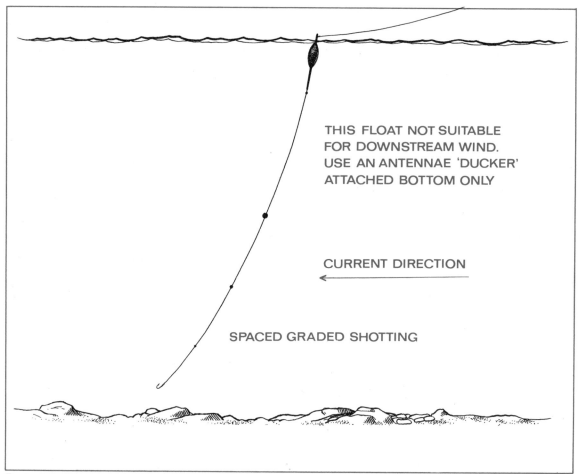

THIS FLOAT NOT SUITABLE
FOR DOWNSTREAM WIND.
USE AN ANTENNAE 'DUCKER'
ATTACHED BOTTOM ONLY

CURRENT DIRECTION
←——————————

SPACED GRADED SHOTTING

Typical shallow-water rig for fast streams. Ideal for caster fishing

less than 5 ft. deep.

The tackle should be set to trot down just off the bottom and at the start of the match about a dozen casters are thrown into the swim, slightly downstream. As the float reaches half way down the swim more casters are introduced. At the end of the swim the float is held back and the bait allowed to swing in the current. If there is no response the tackle should be quickly retrieved and the operation repeated. As soon as fish are contacted the spot where the bite occurred should be noted and feed introduced to that position. If the operation goes according to plan the fish congregate in one spot. The trotting-down style is abandoned and the float held back allowing the bait to descend slowly to the gathering shoal. They should be excited by this time and ignore the unfamiliar character-istics of the bait. A hooked fish should not be brought through the swim, but allowed to drop back and drawn towards the angler without disturbing the rest of the shoal. Dace too, react in this manner, but overfeeding tends to force shoals of both roach and dace further down the swim and they are often lost by the angler who is over-zealous with his feeders.

In the winter and in times of flood the caster can be fished lying on the bottom. In these circumstances groundbait helps to get the feed quickly down to the fish. Quality roach often fall to the caster when fished in this style in the winter.

A fast water is difficult to plumb thoroughly. Once the depth has been gauged directly in front of the angler trial and error methods can be used to indicate the nature of the bottom. Any doubts must be overcome with the use of the plummet.

Deeper water must be fished in heavier style. The large Avon-style float is ideal, but best used in an upstream wind. There is little to beat a large ducker float used with the line attached to the bottom ring only to overcome downstream wind. For distance and control in casting, well spaced-out shot are required. But they should be slightly heavier than those mentioned earlier. They are graduated down the line, the largest being furthest away from the hook. Group shotting is useful when a long tail is used for certain types of chub fishing. In fast choppy water the group keeps the bait down at the required level and often positive bites are obtained.

Deep fast waters cannot be fished with a fixed float and here the slider proves its value. This time the small eye is near to the top of the float at right angles to the body so that the normal line position from the top of the float can still be used. Conditions have to be favourable for this style and often legering is the best style in deep waters. Tackle can be similar to the link leger used on drains, but the method of detection differs. The swing tip is replaced with the quiver tip. This is a thin piece of fibre glass with two rod rings for the line and it has a screw end similar to the swing tip.

In effect the quiver tip is a stiff swing tip and the same methods used with the swing tip should be adopted. The target board is particularly useful, but mainly as a bite detector and not as a wind break.

When the cast has been made the line is tightened against the leger lead, which should be just heavy enough to hold the bottom. This bends the tip slightly round. If a fish moves the lead the bite will be instantly indicated. Other bites result in a definite movement of the tip towards the far bank. With practice every little knock can be seen and they indicate exactly what is happening to the bait.

Some anglers have found the fine tips of their match rods good bite indicators for legering. They have painted the ends and watch for the slightest movement against a target board. Another method of bite detection is to hold the line between the fingers. Every touch can be felt, although on really cold days the fingers lose some of their sensitivity.

Whichever method is chosen, groundbaiting must again be accurate and it is always difficult to gauge accurately where the bait is landing. If it is found that the fish are responding well down the swim, it is obvious the groundbait is taking too long to reach the bottom. The only remedy is to stiffen the groundbait mixture.

If deep water does not produce many fish it must be remembered that the sides of the river often contain small roach and dace. Tackle for catching them can be very light and the loose feeding tactics described for the shallow water will shoal the fish. It is surprising how many matches are won by the angler who concentrates on the small fish near the bank.

On many of the bigger waters, especially in the summer, the bleak is quite easy to find. Because it is so small it is despised by many, but it can bring prizes when nothing else is feeding. The bleak is a surface feeding fish and as speed is essential if a good weight is to be made, no reel is used. The finest rod for this fishing is the lightweight roach pole that can be bought for a couple of pounds or less. An ideal length is from 16–18 ft.

Constant introduction of feeders brings bleak into the swim. Tackle should be very light. Two small shot, or perhaps even one, can be used. Bites are extremely fast, but once a good shoal has been gathered, watching the float can be forgotten. Simply cast, count three and strike. There should be a fish hanging on. It is essential to keep the bait moving.

Maggots are the best bait for bleak and by using the tough commercial type it is possible to catch several fish on one maggot, so saving valuable time.

I have found a very effective way of catching bleak is to allow the float to lie flat on the surface. This gives a better indication of each bite. Barbless hooks are easier to remove but a tight line must always be kept, otherwise the fish can drop off. My own personal record is 15 lb. of bleak; well over 300 fish in five hours.

Summary

I have discussed a variety of techniques for different waters. Several of the points made must be adhered to for all matches. There must be consistent baiting of the swim. Whether it be with loose maggots or groundbait it should be introduced regularly if a feeding shoal of fish is to be held. Even when fish are being caught, feeding must continue.

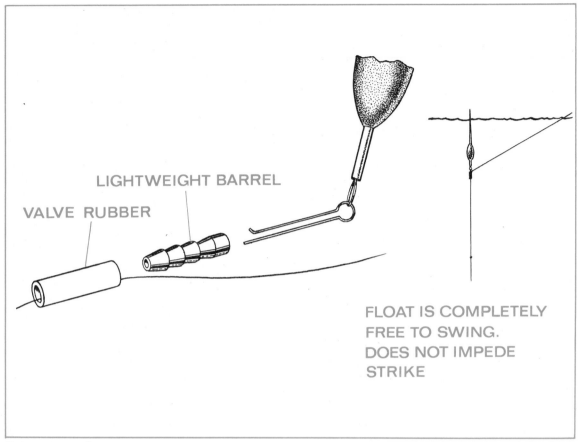

VALVE RUBBER

LIGHTWEIGHT BARREL

FLOAT IS COMPLETELY
FREE TO SWING.
DOES NOT IMPEDE
STRIKE

Quick-change float attachment

Shotting is important, being the means by which the bait is presented naturally. Although set patterns have been described, the individual should understand that variations can be tried.

Speed is essential, but never rush. More haste, less speed, is a good maxim to observe. Above all, every action should be smooth.

Be prepared to change tackle if things do not go well. A method which does not bring fish must be abandoned. Experience and knowledge from previous matches can often be put to good use with tackle changes.

It is a good idea to use a method of float attachment that enables a quick change to be made without disturbing the terminal tackle. One of the best of several popular methods is to use the attachment illustrated. This can be used whether the float is attached to the bottom of the float or both the top and bottom.

Finally, pre-match preparation is vitally important. Bait can be perfect provided ample time is given to its preparation, and tackle should be given a thorough check every week. Floats should be well varnished and plenty of hooks must be available. There should be ample line on the reel, the last few yards used in the previous match should be discarded in case of weakness. Rod ferrules must fit easily, but check that wear has not made them loose. Each item is checked into the basket or box so that nothing is forgotten. Make sure there are no weaknesses in the mesh of either keep net or landing net.

Rods can be given a coat of silicone polish. This keeps the water off and helps to prevent the line sticking to the rod. After the match, nets and any other wet items should be put out to dry.

(Opposite) An umbrella will provide shelter not only from rain, but also from wind and sun

Jack P. Tupper

Fish Baits for Sea Fishing

Alive or dead, whole or in pieces, there's no denying that fish is an excellent and deservedly popular bait. But having said that, there are many other points at issue. Which species are most attractive as bait, and of these which are best presented whole and which should be cut up and how?

When considering bait of this type one immediately thinks of the more commercial fish. Those that are available direct from the fishmonger's slab, for example, mackerel, herrings and sometimes pilchards. These particular fish are attractive because they exude oil from their flesh, particularly when they are cut up for bait.

This chapter also deals with those other species which are fairly readily available, e.g. eels, smelt, whitebait, small bream (sometimes called chad), pouting, etc., and suggests suitable ways in which they can be used.

When should a whole fish be used?

There is considerable argument as to the merits of using a whole fish or a fillet, particularly when angling for large skate, tope and conger, but consider first the manner in which a large fish will take a bait.

Initially it will seize it crosswise in its mouth and move some distance before turning and beginning to gorge the bait, which it normally does head first. The bait is taken in this manner presumably to avoid the spines and the natural 'scrub' of the scales of the captive fish. It appears that a boned fillet of fish is far more likely to be seized quickly, and with confidence.

One would have thought that a fish would have been quite happy to accept a whole fish as bait, as this is certainly a more natural bait form.

However, it appears that with the removal of the backbone, even with a large steel hook substituted, one's chances of a catch improves considerably especially when one is considering the larger members of the species. It is interesting to note that some of the largest conger eels taken during the last few years have all been lured by a bait from which the backbone had been removed.

In my opinion possibly the only exception to this rule is when fishing for shark when the bait is fished on float tackle. Under these conditions a whole fish such as a mackerel, herring, or pilchard, seems a more natural prey.

Is there a special way to hook either whole fish, or large fillets?

There are several methods in which this can be done but in nearly all cases it is necessary to use a baiting needle. Where a whole mackerel or similar whole fish is to be used for bait, one hook is required with a trace about ten inches long. This is drawn into position by the baiting needle which is put into the eye of the mackerel and threaded along the backbone and brought out near the tail. The second hook which is mounted on a slightly shorter wire snood is inserted in the opposite flank so that the two loops of the separate snoods are brought up together, each hook is taking an equal share of the weight of the bait. The wire should be seized or tied with thread or elastic cotton at the tail end, and a six or eight foot wire trace is then clipped onto the

(opposite) A fighting conger comes to the gaff. By far the most successful bait for this species, is fish in one form or another

(above) The day's catch. A good mixed bag of cod, coalfish, and gurnard

(opposite) A good tope is weighed ashore. When angling for this species, fish baits reign supreme

(right) A freshly caught mackerel, wire trace, and tempered steel hook—an ideal bait for big conger

two loops of the hook snoods. If only one hook is required it is probably best to insert this into the mouth of the bait and thread the trace up through it and out at the tail. Again, use a binding to prevent the mackerel slipping down the wire and bunching on the hook.

Fillets of fish can be mounted in a similar manner. However, always hook the tail section first. This can be fixed to the eye of the hook with a small lashing. This enables the bait to move in the tide and present an attractive appearance. And this, it must be remembered, is the most important fact of all. To be successful both fillets and whole fish must be presented in an attractive and lifelike manner. Always avoid partially covering the point of the hook and giving the appearance of something totally unnatural.

Fillets can be cut long and thin giving an appearance of sand eels; hook these at the tail end where the skin of the fish is the toughest, and when fishing for smaller species, thread the hook in and out to make it secure.

Mackerel last

Can one use small pieces of fish?

The flesh of mackerel, pilchard and herring is used extensively for bait, after the fish has been filleted, and cut into diagonal strips. By far the best section of bait is the triangular section closest to the tail where the skin is toughest; this is generally known as a last or lask.

A last, cut as a spinning bait from the tail of a mackerel, is particularly good for drift-lining. Hook as shown in the illustration, as it then presents a very natural appearance.

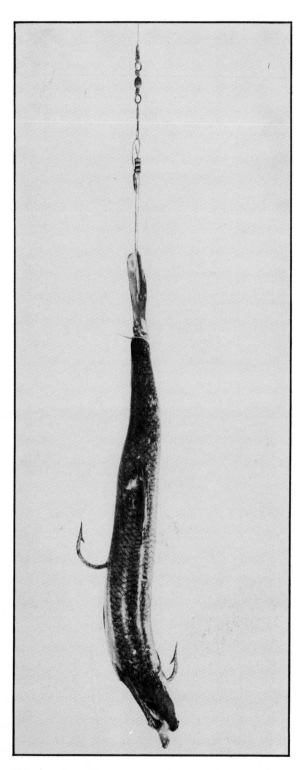

Two-hook tackle used with mackerel bait

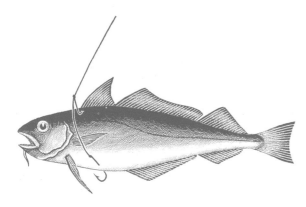

Pouting used as livebait

The diagonally cut sections of fish from the fillet should be hooked by inserting the point of the hook in the skin side and out through the flesh; the bait is then twisted and the hook again taken through, skin side first. Treated in this manner the maximum amount of flesh is shown, and what oils there are, attract other fish.

Which species of fish can be used as bait?

There are numerous small fish which can be used as bait, either whole or cut into smaller pieces, and possibly the most popular are sand eels, smelt, whitebait, chad, pouting, and wrasse.

Pouting or whiting pout are generally quite easily caught and can be used with great success either whole or in fillets for conger, skate, and tope.

In recent years, live pouting have been used with considerable success for bass fishing. Although this bait is not generally used, a number of bass anglers have noted that the larger of the species, when taken, invariably contain a pouting in the stomach. As a result, live pouting have been fished in much the same manner as the coarse angler uses livebaits for pike. The main state, and cannot be trailed as a deadbait as their possibly through the lips depending on whether or not there is any tide flow. It has generally been found that pouting can only be used in the live state, and cannot be trailed as a deadbait as their body shape makes them twist in a manner which is not attractive to the bass.

Chad, or the small specimens of sea bream, generally black bream, either whole or filleted, make a good conger bait. They should be scaled before being used.

Small wrasse also attract conger and they are often used with great success when harbour fishing for bass. Wrasse are very often taken in lobster pots or nets and when dead are thrown over the side, along with the offal and other waste which accumulates on professionals' boats. This waste will attract bass and in so doing they will come to accept wrasse as a natural food.

Whitebait

Whitebait is a term which varies according to the area. Nevertheless, whitebait or brit are probably the most common names used to describe the intermingled fry of herrings, pilchards, sprats, and sometimes mackerel, which vary in size from almost microscopic proportions to

The correct method of hooking bunches of small baitfish

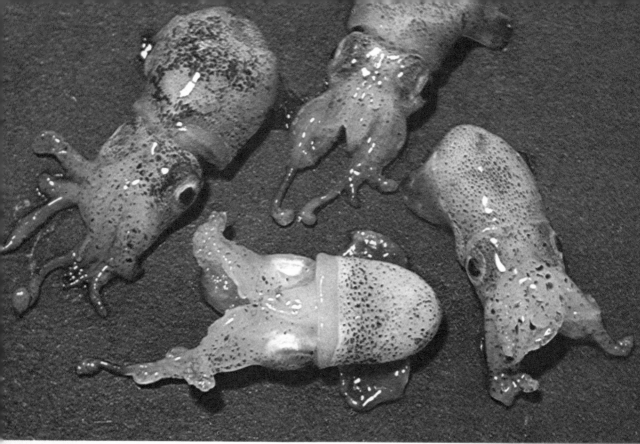

(top) Young squid. When adult these will prove to be extremely effective baits for conger, skate, and tope

(bottom) Cockles make a good stand-by bait for pouting and flatfish but their toughness may result in fewer bites than when the more popular baits are used

about two inches in length. Shoals of whitebait or brit are sought after by larger bass, mackerel and some other species. On occasions when they find shoals of brit they feed voraciously. At times like this the angler may either be successful in making a very good kill, or, as sometimes happens, have great difficulty in even hooking one fish.

As bait, whitebait are very delicate, and are generally far too fragile to be kept alive. They can be extremely attractive to bass or mackerel fished either on float tackle or on a fine drift-line. Alternatively, for larger species, fish them in bunches close to the bottom and hook the dead fish through the eyes. Use a fine hook, but even so you will find that it is generally impossible to cast these baits any distance.

What is the difference between sprats and whitebait?

The general term whitebait, as previously mentioned, does in fact include the fry of sprats. However, whereas the fry of herrings and pilchards tend to disperse into deeper water later in the year, sprats are still taken by net fishermen having reached a size of only two to three inches. During the autumn and winter they are easily obtained from fish shops or from inshore fishermen who are engaged in the 'sprat trade'. They make very good cod and whiting bait, and in areas where sprats are abundant, it is quite useless to use any other bait form during the sprat season. Like whitebait, they tend to be rather soft, but nevertheless they can be hooked through the mouth and out through the belly, or by running the hook into the mouth, out through the gill and then driving the hook point through the body. Pollack and bass will also take sprats if they are fished on a drift-line.

What are smelts and can they be used as bait?

The smelt is a small, slim-bodied, fork-tailed, big-eyed fish with rather large scales. There are two types, namely the atherine or sand smelt, and the true smelt. Both species are transparent and have a greenish-brown or grey back which is dusted with tiny black dots. They are also

Feeding seagulls are frequently a tell-tale sign that small fry are feeding on, or just below, the surface. It is also a good indication that the fry are being driven to the surface by mackerel or bass

103

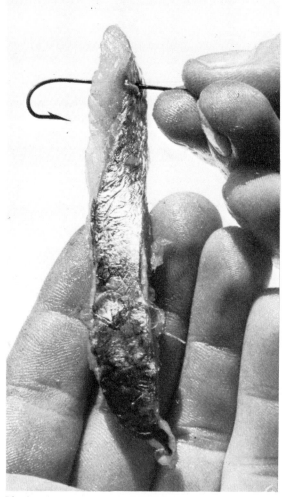

Placing herring strip on a long-shanked hook—a fine bait for cod, pollack, red bream, and ling

This small creature, known as a shanny (or Blennius pholis) is a bait that is often worth using for bass wherever it is found

occasionally known as the cucumber smelt because of the faint cucumber-like smell which exudes from freshly caught fish. Whole smelt are particularly attractive to bass, and if used alive, can be hooked in a similar manner to live pouting. They are easily damaged however, and have a very limited life.

Are sand-eels a popular bait?

Sand-eels are considered by many anglers, particularly those who fish for bass, to be among the finest baits there are. It has been proved that they can be taken great distances to areas where sand-eels are not normally found, and still be used with deadly effect. There are two types of

sand-eel around our coasts, the lesser, and the greater. The lesser sand-eel grows to about four inches in length, while the greater sand-eel is often two or three times as long. They both have the ability to burrow into the sand with remarkable speed, and the unfortunate thing from the angler's point of view is that the areas where they are found are very limited. There may be miles of sandy beach but not one sand-eel.

The sand-eel forms a part of the natural food of a considerable number of fish e.g. bass, pollack, skate, turbot, and cod. In areas where they are plentiful they are used by commercial fishermen as bait on long lines. The main difficulty, as with many baits, is in obtaining them.

How are sand-eels caught?

The most efficient method is by using a fine-meshed seine net, and sand-eels caught in this way usually live the longest. In certain areas along the coast Local Fishery Officers have designated areas where sand-eel seines may be used. For as one can appreciate, the mesh is much smaller than the average seine net, and care must always be taken when using these nets to return to the water the small immature fish of other species.

In some areas, anglers own nets jointly; this helps to cut the initial expense which is high. But with the introduction of modern fibres such as terylene and nylon, the nets have now become virtually indestructible and therefore their life is spread over many years.

Seine net fishing for eels is similar to ordinary sand or beach seine fishing. The net is 'shot' from the stern of a boat in a semi-circle, and the ends drawn ashore by the ropes attached. The sand-eels in the area being gathered into the bag of the net. When bringing a sand-eel seine ashore, care must be taken to treat the contents of the bag as gently as possible. The eels should always be deposited initially into a watertight box approximately half filled with sea water. Check that weavers are not amongst the catch.

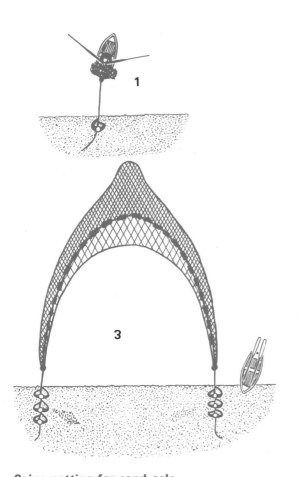
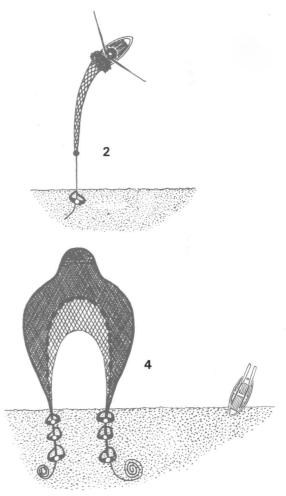

Seine netting for sand-eels

1. Net loaded into dinghy, one man securing shore end

2. Net payed-out from stern of dinghy

3. Net hauled from shore

4. Haul near completion, note the ends are brought nearer to each other as the net is retrieved

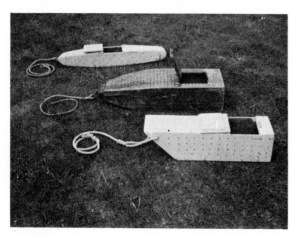

Three types of penner for the storing or transportation of sand-eels

The weaver is a small, poisonous-spined fish which lives in sand similar to that occupied by sand-eels. The depositing of the freshly caught sand-eels in the box also has the added advantage that all the liveliest baits will immediately swim to the top of the water and can be poured off with some of the sea water into the courges or penners in which they are to be stored. The remainder of the contents of the box can be sorted, and the sand-eels that have suffered crushing or similar damage whilst in the net can be stored in a bucket for future use as ground-bait or for use as deadbait.

Where there are sand-eels they are usually abundant. And apart from netting, they can be dug with a small hand-fork from along the low water mark, or scraped from the sand, near or on the edge of the water, with a wire hook about one and a half inches in diameter. The eels are hooked out with a scraper and quickly picked up by the free hand. As with so many other things, skill is acquired by practice, but even so, the eels, having been handled, do not live as long as those taken by seine net.

Why are sand-eels not kept in a bucket or wooden box for any length of time?

Although it is quite possible to keep sand-eels in a plastic bucket or wooden box for a short period they would soon die if left. The best method of keeping them is in a penner or courge; the method of constructing and using them is dealt with in another chapter of this book. Sand-eels cannot be contained in metal buckets or tins, particularly if the former is galvanised.

How are sand-eels used as bait?

If tidal conditions are extremely slack, the eel may be hooked through the skin on its back and then allowed to swim freely either on a drift-line or float tackle. If there is any appreciable amount of tide the hook should be inserted either through the upper lip only, or through the head in the lower corner of the eye. In spite of this apparently lethal operation, the eels live for a considerable time, but excessive handling will soon kill them. An alternative method for hooking a sand-eel is by passing the hook through the mouth and out of the gills and hooking it into the skin of the belly. It has been found however, that sand-eels hooked in this manner will not live as long as those hooked through the base of the eye. This method may appear inhuman but in fact there is nothing under the base of the eye at this point, and the hook merely rides on the eye socket. As the majority of those fish that feed on sand-eels swallow them head first, it is obviously better to keep the hook as near to the front of the eels as possible.

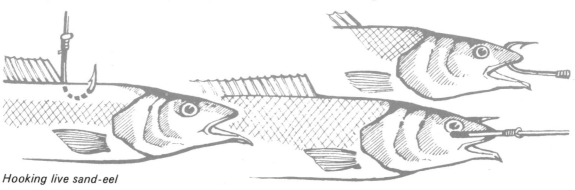

Hooking live sand-eel

(top) An unusual catch. Three of the six species of gurnard to be caught around our coast: tub gurnard (top), grey gurnard (centre), and red gurnard (bottom)

(bottom) The result of a successful day's offshore fishing. A good catch of cod, pollack, ling, and red bream

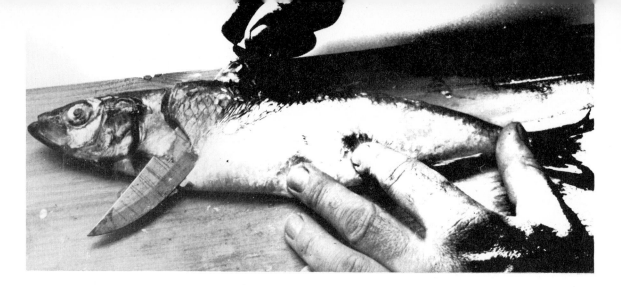

(above) Taking a lask from the flank of a herring. This is a fish bait that holds an attraction for many species

(below) Two baits for the price of one. A 1¾ lb. mackerel containing nineteen sand eels

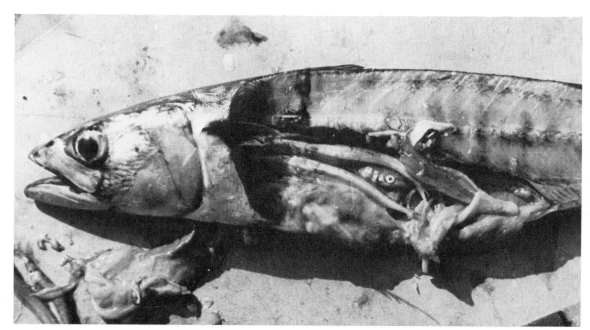

Dead sand-eels can be hooked in a similar manner to live eels and used on a drift-line. But when fished on bottom tackle they are probably best hooked by passing the hook through the mouth and out at the gills and then set into the skin at the base of the belly.

If the sand-eel slips down the hook shank and tends to 'bunch' on the bend, try tying the sand-eel's lip just above the eye of the hook with a piece of cotton or thread.

Some anglers suggest hooking the sand-eel through the lips or through the lower jaw, but if the bait is to be cast any distance and is hooked in this manner, it will tear free.

Can other small fish be used as bait?

There is really no limit to the type of small fish that can be used as bait. Skate and conger eel will at times accept almost any small fish. Gobies and blennies have been used with success for bass and pollack, and even that unattractive-looking fish, the bullhead, should not be ignored.

Sand dabs and plaice are often used as tope bait, but these are generally more successful if they are mounted on the hook in a special way. Remove the head and then cut along the centre

Flatfish used as bait

of the backbone on the upper side. This enables the fish to be folded or rolled into a tube, and is kept in this position by two or three pieces of light twine.

The hook which has previously been put through the shoulder of the fish projects clear of the barb and is virtually inside the 'tube'. Attach the trace to the tail of the flatfish by a small piece of twine or thread, this prevents the bait twisting out of shape on the hook mounting.

It is difficult to assess all the reasons why the tope prefers the flatfish mounted in this way, but it is certainly more distinguishable, the white flesh of the underside shows up very well on the sandy or muddy sea bed. The removal of its head is necessary to enable the body to be rolled, and in any event this also allows a certain amount of blood to be washed into the water which adds to the attraction.

Is there an advantage in using a bait that has been cut and allowed to bleed?

It is generally considered by many anglers, especially those who fish for tope, that there is an advantage in lacerating or cutting a fish bait (if it is not a fillet) in order to allow the juices and blood to permeate through the water and thus add to the attraction. Some only remove the head of the fish being used; this has the same effect.

The only disadvantage of using either a fillet or whole fish that has been cut, is that it is easier for crabs or whelks to strip pieces off once the protection of the skin has been lost. It will therefore be found that a lacerated fish tends to disintegrate quite quickly, and it is advisable to use this method only when there is a plentiful supply of bait. Soft and messy baits often cut down your chances of making a good kill.

Can the potential of a fish bait be improved by any other method?

As previously mentioned, it is possible to soak any bait in pilchard oil for a considerable period, but there is little point in soaking a whole fish as the amount that is absorbed is comparatively negligible. However a number of anglers have produced one answer; they insert cotton wool or pieces of sponge which have been soaked in pilchard oil into the mouth of the bait so that the wash of water through the gills produces the desired effect.

In the absence of exhaustive tests carried out over a period of years to establish these points, they should be accepted as improving the chances of catching a fish and therefore advantage should be taken of them wherever possible.

(Above) A beautiful bronze-flanked chub which tipped the scales at 4 lb.

(Top left) Grayling—'the lady of the stream', a fish of autumn

(Left) Where small fish are attracted by the ground-bait, the perch often follow—to feed on the fish!

(Right) Tench—a fish of the more sluggish rivers. These fish averaged 4½ lb.

Colin Gamble

Bait for River Fishing

There are plenty of rivers where there will be ten anglers baiting with maggots or chrysalis for every one who is not. There are indeed, places where the non-maggot man would be out-numbered by as much as a hundred to one.

The majority will tell you, with some truth, that they invariably bait with maggots because it is almost a guarantee that they will catch fish. They would have to agree, however, that maggots as a bait are totally unselective with regard to both species and size of fish caught on them. They appeal to minnows as much as to barbel, to fingerling roach as much as to one-pounders. Although one can sometimes offer maggots selectively by one's choice of swim and method of presentation, there are many occasions when each bite could equally well come from any species and from any size of fish from ounces to pounds in weight.

Maggots then, are a most convenient bait, acceptable to every species and to every size of fish. Their appeal is not seasonal, for many rivers have popular stretches which are just about permanently groundbaited with them. One can think of particular examples where to fish any other bait is almost a waste of time as maggots form the major part of the fish's diet.

Nevertheless, none of this in any way detracts from the virtues of other baits. Indeed, in some instances the very qualities of the maggot provide the reasons for using other baits.

No one who knows about chub for example, will expect them to remain where there is a disturbance caused by the catching of small fish. Lots of fine chub fall to maggot baits, but if

maggots bring small fish it will usually mean that there is little chance of chub remaining. They will have faded away with the first disturbance.

If you intend to catch chub use a bait unlikely to appeal to roach, dace, gudgeon, bleak, etc. Your prospects immediately increase tenfold. Put on a size six or eight hook and a matching bait of bread, cheese, sausage, a couple of lob-worms, a slug, a crayfish, a piece of fat bacon, a strip of tripe, in fact almost anything you like provided it is unlikely to be taken by fish smaller than those you aim to catch.

It is not always an advantage to be using the food the fish are most used to eating. The more commonly used the bait, the more likely the fish are (at least the larger and wiser ones) to associate it with disturbing noises and unpleasant experiences. Hence the value of ringing the changes in baits. It takes a little courage to put it to the test, but it is true that roach and dace will eat wood-lice and earwigs as eagerly as they will maggots, and it is quite certain that they will have no cause at all to regard them with suspicion.

A chub can learn quite early in the season to beware of cheese. In waters where cheese is widely used its effectiveness can have waned by August. The only chub likely to be afraid of a bunch of water snails, for example, will be those which have been hooked on this bait, and these are probably very few.

Cereals of many kinds make clean, simple baits which do well when fished on the bottom for roach, bream and chub. Stewed wheat is well known and takes a lot of beating, but if you con-

Above: A welcome addition to any angler's catch, a 1 lb. roach in prime condition

Below: A 1½ lb. crucian carp is admired. These dogged little fighters give good sport on suitable tackle

sult an obliging corn chandler you will find he stocks a great many items of which only wheat, peas, and hemp have been seriously tried as baits.

Do not waste time and money on oils and essences reputed to make your bait more attractive. If any successful additives exist, which I doubt, their appeal will surely be less than that of a completely natural item of food such as a worm or an insect.

I would be perfectly content if my baits were to be restricted to the bread baits, i.e. flake, paste and crust; to worms, i.e. redworms, brandlings and lobs; plus the items which are to be found in and around the water, i.e. insects, snails, beetles, grass-hoppers, shrimps, grubs, small fish, and so on.

To use a bait of flake, merely tear a piece of crumb from a slice of moist new bread. If the current is lively or the cast long, fold the bread around the hook shank and squeeze it on with thumb and finger, leaving the hook point in the soft, unsqueezed part. In easy currents it is enough merely to squeeze part of the portion and to pass the hook through it.

To use crust, merely tear off a piece of suitable size, remembering that it swells considerably when wet. Pass the hook through from the crust

For how many fish was this their last sight? The formidable jaws of a large pike

side so that it emerges just through the crumb. Very small hooks will tear out of bread baits, but used on a hook of sensible size such baits are effective and durable in all kinds of water.

To make plain bread-paste, and no other is better, except on occasions cheese paste; use stale bread, up to a week old. Remove the crusts, soak in cold water for just a few seconds, take a handful and knead it with the knuckles of the other hand until it is smooth and soft. Good paste must be soft, for fish bite better at soft mouthfuls. If paste stays on the hook through the retrieve it is certainly too firm. If it occasionally leaves the hook on casting, it is probably just right. There is no need to mix in cotton wool or other fibrous matter if paste is properly made.

All kinds of worms are useful, but without question the finest worm bait for general use is the lobworm. It is most easily caught while it lies on the surface of well-established turf on dark, damp nights.

All species of fish will eat lobs sometimes, but this bait is at its most effective in coloured or clearing water. Perch and chub will take them freely in any conditions; tench and bream when they are feeding well. They are always a good bait for barbel. Roach often go very strongly for lob tails about an inch and a half in length, fished hard on the bottom in autumn and winter.

Red worms, bright and vigorous, can be found in the damp conditions under rotting wood, sacking, dead leaves, and so on, and can easily be accumulated by regularly emptying tea leaves into a shady corner. In sizes from one to three inches long they make a splendid bait for any species.

Brandlings, striped red and yellow with a yellow tip to the tail, are to be found in manure and compost heaps. They exude a yellow fluid and an unpleasant smell when touched, but this does not deter fish from eating them greedily.

Many anglers, regarding the bait as the most decisive point of their approach, allow themselves to be diverted from more important things as they search for super baits of infallible appeal, even of secret composition. I very much doubt if they achieve anything by searching.

A simple bait is very rarely to be bettered. The important thing is that it should be well presented in the right place.

(Above) A fine 20 lb. winter pike from the River Watchem

(Below) The Zander, a fish with a growing reputation among big-fish hunters

Colin Gamble

Groundbaiting in Rivers

It is generally accepted that the main purpose of groundbaiting is to attract to the swim fish which are scattered at various distances downstream. This is achieved by maintaining a stream of food particles through the swim. I think though, that it is important to emphasize the words *food particles*. Even though fish may initially be attracted by a clouding of the water, like that produced by using a finely-ground cereal mixture, or mud and sand, the attraction will last only until the fish tire of seeking non-existent food items.

Some groundbaits can be mixed to a very firm consistency so that the action of the water in breaking it up is resisted for a considerable time and the groundbait rolls down the bed in sizeable pieces. This certainly offers food-sized morsels, but it defeats the object of groundbaiting if it encourages feeding on the groundbait when the hook-bait is of a different nature.

I am quite sure that groundbaiting is at its most effective when it not only attracts and concentrates the fish, but when it also accustoms them to feeding on items of the same nature as the hook-bait; when, in fact, it induces some degree of preoccupation with one type of food or one size of food.

This is not a new idea. It was the basis of the mammoth groundbaiting programmes of the last century when, for example, many thousands of lobs were fed into a barbel swim, not primarily to attract barbel, but to accustom them to feeding on lobs. Similarly, the carcass of a sheep was

Opposite: A punt forms a useful platform from which to trot float tackle down a weirpool

hung over the water to shed a steady and prolonged supply of maggots, not so much to attract a shoal, but to ensure that the fish would be pre-conditioned to accept maggots when they were used as bait. There would certainly have been little point in doing this and then using any bait other than maggots.

It is then, very sound practice to groundbait with maggots when fishing with maggot bait, using a cereal mixture as a carrying agent for the maggots when this is necessary to achieve distance. But do not forget that the same effect would be obtained by any other method of getting the maggots to the right spot. By using a catapult, for instance, or the throwing tube, popular in the North. The cloud of fine cereal which accompanies the maggots down the water does not itself increase the chances that fish will accept maggot baits.

If, instead of casting perhaps twenty yards to the swim and having to throw maggots the same distance, one fished from a boat moored above the swim, the maggots could with equal effect, be merely dropped in and left to wash down the current.

Prolonged feeding with maggots is undoubtedly effective in attracting fish and inducing them to feed exclusively on maggots. I am not so sure that it is advisable when fishing for powerful fish like chub and barbel, for it might be wiser to use a bait which would more readily permit the use of a hook and line capable of coping with a larger fish.

I see little point in feeding the fish and then baiting the hook with an item which, for successful presentation, demands a hook of a size which gives the fish more chance of escape than the angler has of making a capture.

In fast, deep water, where loose items are swept away very quickly there is much to be said for the use of a swim feeder or bait dropper so that the feed is carried direct to the bed and released there. The swim feeder remains on the line to let its contents trickle down past the bait; the bait dropper is used only to place the feed, being withdrawn when it has done so. This demands accuracy of placing.

Anglers who fish with hemp seed as bait invariably use it as groundbait also. Yet one can see countless anglers using worms, cheese, wheat, bread, etc., as hook bait while groundbaiting only with the usual finely-ground cereal mixture sold by tackle dealers. I believe these anglers could only profit by keeping in the swim a few samples of the hook bait; for instance a dozen grains of wheat, a few knobs of cheese, half a dozen worms, or some pellets of bread, rather than maintaining a supply of a food of a type quite different from that on the hook.

Worms can be distributed easily if they are enclosed in a paper bag weighted with a stone. The intermittent distribution is an important consideration. It is far better to maintain a trickle of food items than to give larger amounts at wider intervals.

An easy way of observing this principle, when fishing a fast run by the near bank, is to put some roughly broken bread in a keep net, hang it in the current and give it a shake from time to time. This releases a stream of particles similar to the flake or crust bait on the hook.

Pre-feeding is not easy to contrive in rivers as heavy supplies of food are too rapidly dispersed. I have had considerable success, however, with chub and roach in a fairly fast stream by packing an open mesh onion sack with broken bread and weighting it with a couple of building bricks. I have waded out to leave it overnight at the head of a long run to feed out pieces of bread over a long period. Needless to say, the successful baits have been flake or crust, fished well downstream of the sack of bread, and once the right line down the swim has been found it has seemed that the fish were queueing up to take the next bait to travel down the current.

The amount of groundbait needed for full effect depends on many factors. The volume and speed of water give the first indication. The deeper and faster the water, the more groundbait

will be needed and the stiffer it should be mixed. The species to be caught, their size and number, need to be taken into account.

A large river with a good flow which holds a good head of large bream will call for groundbaiting on a scale which would stagger those who are used to smaller, quieter waters. At the other end of the scale there are small streams of little depth and flow, where a walnut-sized piece of groundbait, half a dozen grains of wheat, or a sprinkling of maggots will be ample if put in approximately every ten minutes.

In cold weather less groundbaiting is generally needed. Indeed, it may well be that as cold conditions allow the angler to anticipate more easily where the fish are likely to be, a meagre scattering of bait samples will suffice to start the probably unenthusiastic feeding.

It is important to remember that solid types of food should be used in smaller amounts, not only because they quickly tend to satisfy the fish, but because they stay where they are put. Groundbait mixtures for fast water can usefully be made more solid by adding cooked potatoes, peas, beans or turnip.

Groundbaiting should not be used merely as a habit. There are occasions when the major problem is to succeed in getting a bait to the fish without alarming them. In these cases a handful of groundbait every few minutes might mean that no fish will remain within angling range.

A vital point in all groundbaiting is to ensure that the groundbait and the hook bait are in the same area. Such calculations are not as easy as they sound and many anglers would be surprised if they took more trouble to estimate the time taken for groundbait to sink and the distance it covers while sinking. All too often groundbait thrown out in front of the angler feeds a swim thirty or forty yards away.

All groundbaiting need not be with artificially introduced substances. There is a lot to be said for the old practice of raking up the gravel to send down the current a stream of silt with many larvae, insects, etc. The same result can be achieved by vigorously shaking a weed bed.

The importance of groundbaiting varies from river to river, from swim to swim, and with the season of the year. It may be no more than a snare which diverts attention from factors far more important to success or it may be the one step which brings results.

(Above) Roach from the River Nadder

(Below) A mirror carp is returned to the river. Although found in the slower rivers it is a powerful fighter and can prove more than a match for normal river tackle

Eddie Wood

Choosing a Dinghy

After a house and a car a boat is probably the most expensive item that the average boat fisherman ever buys, this being so, it is wise to give the matter a great deal of thought.

The availability of a mooring may or may not be a problem, to a large extent it depends upon where you live. In the so-called fashionable harbours where a considerable amount of sailing takes place it may be both difficult and expensive, and one always has the problem of malicious damage to consider if the craft is left on a public beach.

Some sea angling clubs have private boat compounds and one might even consider the expense of keeping a boat in a marina as justified and worthwhile. A 12 or 14 ft. clinker-built mahogany craft can be trailed quite easily, but remember to take the weight of your craft into consideration if you intend launching from anywhere but a 'hard'.

Guidance on where and how to keep your boat is usually best obtained from your local club but if you live inland, as many dinghy fishermen do, contact a sea fishing club with a headquarters in the area you intend fishing.

There are many ways in which you can sensibly help yourself, the main point is to realise that mooring problems do exist, and then use common sense to overcome them.

Under reasonable conditions, three or even four lightly clad persons might travel quite safely across a harbour in a 10 ft. dinghy that is a tender to a larger craft. But to expect a similar number of burly duffle-coated anglers complete with rods etc. to set forth on a fishing trip in such a craft is nothing short of sheer lunacy.

I would suggest that for practical fishing purposes one should aim at a 10 ft. boat for one occupant and an additional 2 ft. for each extra person carried. My experience is, that unless the boat is really big, and by this I mean over 20 ft. in length (which is out of the dinghy class), then four is the maximum that can fish in comfort from a small craft. I'm sure that experience will teach you that two is the ideal crew, after that, even in a 14 ft. boat the demand for space can become embarrassing.

There is no doubt that your new circle of friends will offer a great deal of advice. Most of it will be good and some, although still good, will inevitably lean towards what they like to see in a boat; these thoughts may or may not conflict with yours.

Your local sea and shore conditions must play a large part in the calculations you make when choosing a boat, and here a good boatbuilder can be of great help.

A good boatbuilder, in my opinion, is one who is capable of building a boat suitable for the area in which you are going to use it. It could well be that the yard is many hundreds of miles away, indeed, Hampshire friends of mine have had extremely good dinghies built in Scotland.

The whole point is this, a boatbuilder is a specialist craftsman and one who understands the varying demands that will be placed upon him and his finished product, and it is in this measure of understanding that an efficient dinghy design is created.

Boat shows, and naturally I have in mind the International Boat Show which is held in London each January, provide the aspiring buyer with a good opportunity of talking to builders and to some extent forming his own conclusions. But

I would point out that although there are a number of very seaworthy designs, the fact that the boat is seaworthy does not necessarily make it an efficient boat from the point of view of rod and line angling. For example, there are some designs which are absolutely superb for launch-ing through surf and returning in similar con-ditions, and whilst at sea are ideal for operating lobster pots, but in my opinion they tend to be rather low sided, or in other words, they lack sufficient freeboard to be efficient sea angling dinghies.

1. Trailer is unhitched from car and securing ropes removed

2. Trailer and boat rolled down shingle 'hard' towards water

3. Trailer pushed into water until boat floats. Note 3:1 ratio winch for recovering boat. This can also be done by one man but it is easier if the boat is steadied by a second person as it is winched up

4. Whilst holding on to the painter, dinghy is pushed clear of trailer and painter is brought ashore and tied up

5. Trailer recovered

6. To launch this 14 ft. by 6 ft. beam, oak and mahog-any dinghy, took less than ten minutes and was easily managed single-handed

Plaice, a fish sought after for its sporting and cullinary virtues

A beamy 14 ft. clinker-built dinghy, an ideal craft for inshore fishing

Pollack a-plenty! Three caught on the same trace of feathers

Being a traditionalist I certainly favour wooden boats and would suggest that when buying, one should first look at a craft with mahogany planks and oak ribs. The planking should be $\frac{1}{2}$ in. to $\frac{5}{8}$ in. thick with ribs and gunwales of well seasoned oak of substantial proportions. I would always look for a craft that had ribs no more than 6 in. apart and double nailed between each rib. All nails to be of copper.

A good builder will issue a certificate and guarantee which is approved by the Ship and Boatbuilders National Federation.

It is difficult to be precise regarding present-day prices of new boats as devaluation apart, there is always a tendency for the basic cost of hulls to go up. However, depending upon the quality of materials and finish, one can expect to pay anything from about £8 or £10 per foot to as much as £16 per foot.

This may seem to be quite a wide price range but labour costs account for quite a large proportion of these charges, and one must take into consideration that the cheaper boats possibly have only one coat of sealer and two coats of varnish, and also it could well be that only single nailing is used between the ribs. Looking at the more expensive boats, the specifications may stipulate one sealer plus five coats of varnish and even an anti-fouling compound on that part of the boat which will be below water-level. The varnishing and double nailing pushes the labour charges up considerably, but of course the finished craft is also that much better.

The prices that I have mentioned so far do not include oars, anchors and anchor cables etc.

Note the ease with which the trailer is hitched onto the car. The trailer is not harmed by immersion in salt water as long as it is washed down with fresh water after use and all moving parts, such as wheel bearings, kept well greased

Normally a builder quotes a price for the hull and its basic fittings such as fairleads.

If you discover just the boat you are looking for at a boat show, then you're in luck, because you are then buying something that you can actually see. If the boat on display has already been sold then you can enter into a contract with the firm and ask them to build a sister-ship.

Before giving the final instructions ensure that the contract states clearly the size and full specifications of the boat, e.g. the materials to be used in its construction, the price and manner of payment, and a firm delivery date.

Listen carefully to any suggestions the builder may have, and if you decide to incorporate them see that they are listed in the contract.

Whereas wooden craft are built as a single unit, the g.r.p. dinghy is, in broad terms, a production-line job. The modifications and specialised requirements of the individual are in many cases impossible or extremely difficult to incorporate in a g.r.p. construction.

Quite recently several firms have begun to build g.r.p. dinghies which closely resemble the traditional clinker-built craft and, to be fair, some of the criticisms which have been levelled at this type of craft, e.g. 'sitting on' and not 'in' the water, have to some extent been overcome.

The fact remains that at this time they are not as popular as the traditional boat, but if, as we seem to do in so many things, we follow the American trend, then the future will belong to the g.r.p. craft as on price alone they will tend to dominate the market.

If the boat is not to be a new one then obviously it will be second, third, fourth, or maybe even fifth or sixth-hand. You would be amazed at the number of fifty or even sixty-year-old boats which still change hands at prices far greater than they were originally.

Coats of glistening paint and varnish which can keep a craft looking smart and in good condition, can also hide a multitude of sins. Without doubt the most efficient and safest way of ensuring that the boat you intend buying is sound is to employ the services of a qualified marine surveyor, but, if one thinks about this and then equates the value of the boat and the surveyors charges it will soon be seen that after one or two surveys one would be financially better off to buy a new boat. Marine surveyors

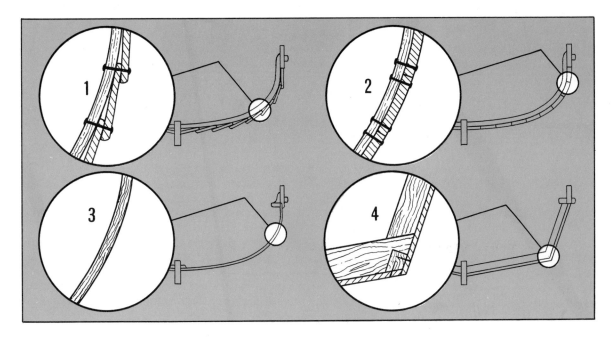

Methods of dinghy construction

1. *Clinker-built construction, each plank overlaps its neighbour*
2. *Carvel-built construction, each plank butts up to its neighbour giving a smooth surface*
3. *Moulded construction, sheets of thin veneer, glass fibre or other plastic materials, are moulded and bonded together*
4. *Hard chine construction, usually built of marine ply, the sides make a distinct angle with the bottom*

are an absolute necessity when buying a large craft but in my opinion, it is hardly practical to employ them when buying a used dinghy valued at about £100. No, one must rely upon common sense and a knowledge of a few tricks of the trade.

If the boat offered for sale is what I call a genuine and rot-free craft then the owner will have no objection to your making a fairly detailed examination. I would suggest that you use the tip of a penknife blade to test the wood. Pay special attention to the boat's ribs, make sure they are not cracked or split. Look carefully for 'tingles' or patches which cover splits or other damage beneath the waterline. A boat that has been out of the water for some time may have begun to warp, and the planking split away from the stem.

To a very large extent the examination of a small craft is plain common sense, and whilst in broad terms I say beware of the painted craft there are a number of boat owners, who for various reasons, have always painted their craft. In fact I know a number of local authorities who stipulate that their safety boats shall be painted when delivered new. It could be they feel a white boat is more conspicuous, or it could be that in their opinion paint is more durable.

However, many, including myself, think that a good yacht varnish is the best material for protecting the timbers as it always retains an amount of elasticity. With the banging and general knocking about that a fishing dinghy sustains it has been proven to my satisfaction that varnish lasts longer and generally speaking, looks smarter.

Inevitably one will think about the new synthetic varnishes which have an extremely hard finish, here again, although this covering is absolutely superlative when used on a racing hull and on many other surfaces, I have found that the knocks and bangs associated with fishing tends to crack and chip a finish of this type. Therefore, my choice remains a good yacht varnish.

Relatively few dinghies are fitted with inboard engines, in fact in a craft of less than 14 ft. the amount of space that an inboard engine takes up is out of all proportion to its value, consequently in this sphere the outboard engine reigns supreme.

Nevertheless, should you be contemplating buying a second-hand craft which is fitted with an inboard propulsion unit then I would suggest that it is examined by a qualified mechanical engineer. But you can make sure that the engine starts easily and runs smoothly and also check that the exhaust pipe and silencer are in good condition; not being patched with an asbestos bandage. That section of the exhaust which runs inboard must be securely fastened and not leak fumes and water into the craft.

Check the amount of play between the propeller shaft and the stern tube and make sure that all the main fixings, for example where the shaft is coupled to the engine and where the engine is bolted down on the bearers, are in good condition and not held by nuts and bolts that are almost rusted away.

To discover the amount of wear that is left in the clutch and the general condition of the engine, is a job for the expert; but it may well be worth-while just withdrawing the oil dip-stick to

A small outboard suitable for powering small dinghies. The propeller can be swung up to avoid damage in shallow water

see if there is any water in with the oil. In short, never buy a pig in a poke.

In my experience the vast majority of dinghy fishermen employ a Seagull engine as a power unit. There are others, for example, British Anzani, Evinrude, Chrysler, etc.; all good and efficient engines, but for general sea angling from a dinghy, the British Seagull engine is certainly by far the most popular. It is used by possibly 80 to 90 per cent of the dinghy fishermen in the part of the country that I know best.

If you are buying a new unit and need detailed advice, then write to the company concerned stating very clearly what you expect the engine to do, and give the dimensions of your craft. For example, you might say that your craft is 12 ft. long, has a 5 ft. beam draught, is clinker (or carvel) built, and the depth of the transom is 'X'. (This measurement tells whether or not you need a long shaft model). Information regarding tidal currents is also helpful, and when allied to the other details it will enable the engine builders to give you the best possible advice.

If you buy a second-hand power unit then go to a reputable dealer, or failing that, have the engine you intend buying inspected by a firm that specialises in the servicing of that particular make. Always remember that in the final analysis a faulty motor can mean your life.

Finally, a word about insurance. There are certain companies who specialise in marine insurance and you will find that, in broad terms, they will all be very loath to give fully comprehensive cover to a craft that is left on a public beach or on a mooring that anyone can reach when the tide goes out. Vandalism is so rife that insurance companies are steadily becoming more and more wary of this type of risk, and in fact, it has been the experience of many of my friends that the companies will only insure their craft if they are kept on private property and/or trailed to and from the launching spot. If the boat is kept on private land then one can expect to pay from about £8 to £12 a year for a fully comprehensive policy covering some three to four hundred pounds' worth of boat and engine and general equipment.

Third-party cover is also very important, some companies give cover up to £25,000 and if you shop around you may find those which give a very handsome no claims bonus.

Cover of this sort should not be neglected.

Eddie Wood

Equipment for Dinghy Fishing

We now come to the equipment and accessories which should either form part of the boat's permanent inventory, or always taken aboard before putting to sea.

Whether or not the boat is fitted with an inboard or an outboard engine a pair of oars together with a matching pair of rowlocks should always be carried; in fact many people carry three oars. Do make sure though that the oars match the boat and that the rowlocks fit snugly into their 'plates'. Too long or too short oars allied to rowlocks that slop about are an abomination and extremely dangerous.

Stow the oars away when not in use, but make certain that they can be readily unshipped, as when you need them you'll need them in a hurry! Have them secured by a lanyard to each rowlock which in turn is secured to one of the thwarts.

On even the smallest of fishing dinghies a folding spray hood is a good investment which offers protection against wind and spray in 'dirty' conditions.

A really strong Sampson post running down through the foredeck, or similar strong securing point is essential, as rough seas throw a lot of strain on the fittings to which the anchor cable is secured.

The anchor cable should be of adequate size and length, bearing in mind the depth of water

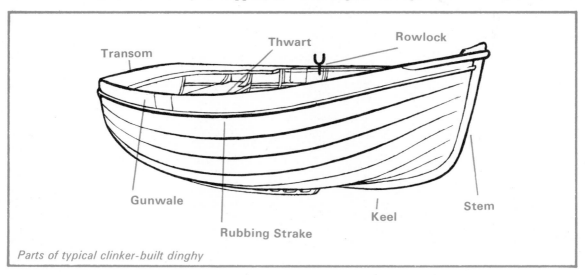

Transom Thwart Rowlock

Gunwale Keel Stem

Rubbing Strake

Parts of typical clinker-built dinghy

normally encountered in the area you fish. As a rough guide, a 14 or 16 ft. boat should always carry a minimum of 20 fathoms (120 ft.) of 1½ in. or 2 in. rope, preferably the larger as it is easier to grip. In my opinion some of the ropes constructed from man-made fibres tend to be 'slimy' when wet, I would suggest that you choose a 'rougher' material.

Fit a fathom of medium chain between the anchor and its cable, this not only substantially increases the holding power of the anchor, but it also reduces the wear on the rope when over a rough bottom.

There are several types of anchor but for general purposes I would recommend the 'Fisherman' pattern, the usual rule being 1 lb. weight of anchor per foot length of boat. It is also useful to carry a 'grapnel' as they are more easily 'broken out' of a rocky sea bed.

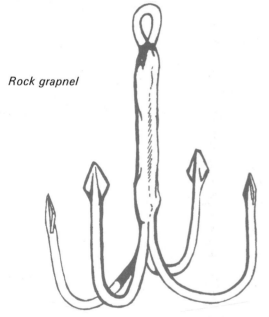

Rock grapnel

Always carry a bailing can on board, even if a bilge pump is fitted, and get into the habit of carrying a reserve can of fuel. Outboard motors, unless fitted with long-range tanks, carry a limited amount of fuel. For example, one of the larger popular makes cruises for approximately 1½ hours on the fuel carried in its standard tank.

(Opposite) An ideal garment for dinghy fishing. Completely waterproof and light in weight, it incorporates an inflatable life-jacket

This may only be sufficient to get you out to your chosen mark. It can be a tricky business refuelling an outboard engine in rough weather, therefore be wise and carry your reserve supply in a maker's recommended container.

It is of the greatest importance always to carry a small kit of tools plus a few spares, e.g. one or two spare plugs, high tension lead, a shear spring and possibly a throttle cable. These items are inexpensive but are invaluable in time of need.

Regarding plugs, and on most outboard engines these are the biggest cause of malfunctions, never carry old ones as spares, if you do you will eventually rue the day you packed them.

Keep your emergency kit plus spanner, screwdriver and pliers, rolled in an oily cloth and packed into a polythene bag. It is also a wise precaution to carry a spare starting cord.

A compass is another 'must', even the small pocket type will do, but when using it stand well clear of the engine or you will get a false reading.

Distress flares and smoke signals can be bought quite reasonably, from ships' chandlers, and as they are often sealed in plastic bags they can be kept dry even in the smallest dinghy. A whistle is a surprisingly effective way of drawing the attention of neighbouring boats' crews if you're in trouble and a small fire extinguisher is a wise investment where petrol engines are concerned. The extinguisher can be fitted inside the casing of an inboard engine or clipped on the underside of a thwart if an outboard is used.

One item of the utmost importance is a first aid kit; I would recommend a ready packed kit, the type you would keep in a car.

Dinghies of g.r.p. construction usually have built-in buoyancy tanks, but if they are not fitted in your boat it is a fairly simple matter to fill the space between one or two thwarts and the bottom boards with foam blocks. The addition of these blocks may not materially improve the buoyancy of an upturned or filled inboard engined boat but it will make all the difference to one fitted with an outboard motor.

Never consider it 'sissy-ish' to wear a life-jacket whilst at sea. There's not much point being a good swimmer if you're tipped overboard in rough conditions some four or five miles from land! Modern jackets, especially the inflatable type, are not all that cumbersome and indeed offer an added protection against cold weather.

An admiring glance for a plump dinghy-caught cod

Trolling for bass in shallow water, here the baited spoon can prove deadly

A pollack caught on light spinning tackle

Gaffing the smaller species is difficult and unnecessary, a landing net is useful in these circumstances

An ideal arrangement of compass, echo sounder, and outboard motor. Everything is within easy reach of the 'skipper'

Three valuable aids to navigation—a graph-type echo-sounder, a prismatic hand-bearing compass, and a large-scale Admiralty chart

Dress warmly and well when you go afloat; a couple of good thick sweaters topped with a wind and waterproof anorak will keep out much of the cold and a woollen hat is not only worn because it looks 'boaty', it serves the purpose of keeping your head and the back of your neck warm, and is not easily blown off.

Keeping your feet warm and dry is important and whilst in general terms I am not in favour of wearing rubber boots at sea, circumstances alter cases: canvas shoes are not much good during November and December. I would suggest that slightly over-large rubbers be worn, and possibly fitted with an inner sole cut from a strip of expanded polystyrene. This allied to a thick pair of woolly socks will do much to keep your feet and legs warm. If an approved life-jacket is worn then your boots will not drag you down in the event of any mishap whilst afloat.

Over-trousers and a jacket made from a strong waterproof material are essential and with a sou'wester to complete the outfit you will be amply protected against the weather. Ankle-length oilskin or plastic coats are in my opinion an encumbrance in a small boat.

For those rare sun-drenched days, a floppy, wide brimmed hat, or peaked cap, will help to prevent you getting a 'boiled lobster' appearance and I find that a pair of polaroid sun-glasses are invaluable.

An Irish skate of 128 lb. Such fish will soon pinpoint any weaknesses in the angler's tackle and sometimes even the angler's arms!

Bruce McMillen

Competitive Sea Angling Methods

What a scope there is here for the angler to use his ingenuity. If an original idea, which may feasibly enhance your chances of catching fish, suddenly comes into your head, don't just forget it. Work on it and try it out. It may well result in your winning more than one competition.

Anglers have plenty to learn, and I am firmly convinced that there are still many methods of presenting enticing baits to the fish which have yet to be discovered, so never become fettered by old and hide-bound ideas. The result of your own new thinking may prove to be an idea for which anglers have been waiting for years. Fish are quite unpredictable creatures, and also being singularly uncommunicative, the darned things simply will not tell us what they want, so it's up to us to try to find out.

Many of the age-old, tried and tested methods are, with some slight modifications, successfully employed to this day. The paternoster, for instance, will still take its toll of fish, as also will the leger. Similarly, the old-style rubber sand-eel, a simply made, relatively cheap lure, can often hold its own against some of the more recently evolved spinners of which there is such a bewildering variety on the market. It has been said, with perhaps more than a measure of truth, that some of these spinners are more likely to attract the angler, than the fish. However, there is not the least doubt that you will be well advised to confine yourself to the few spinners which prove to be real fish catchers, rather than to amass a costly, and often useless collection.

(opposite) Power applied steadily throughout the cast will send this angler's bait way out into the evening tide to where the fish are feeding

One technique that has proved particularly successful involves the use of the baited spoon, a method devoted almost exclusively to the catching of flatfish, bass, and eels. It was perfected by the late John Garrad, ('Seangler') whose book on the subject is commended to all sea anglers interested in inshore fishing. This book gives every essential detail of the procedure, to which Mr. Garrad devoted an appreciable portion of his lifetime, both testing and developing. The baited spoon technique basically involves the use of a baited hook which is closely linked to a metal or plastic spoon. The term, 'baited spoon' may, therefore, be perhaps something of a misnomer, for it is the hook which is baited and not the spoon. Nevertheless, the addition of the spoon to the bait most certainly proves more attractive to the fish, and Mr. Garrad's work on this technique is a typical example of what the angler can do to improve his catches, simply by developing an idea rather than

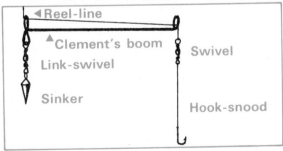

Simple form of running leger using a Clement's boom. This is an effective terminal rig for many species of bottom feeding fish. The boom helps to prevent the bait from becoming entangled with the weight during and after casting, the weight of the sinker can easily be varied to suit changes of tide

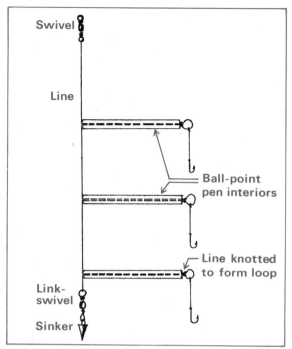

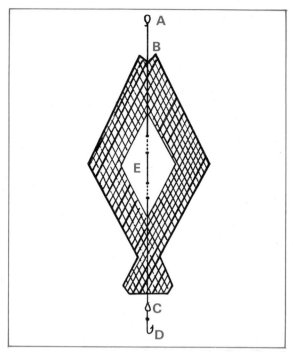

A three-hook paternoster. The line is doubled through each spreader and is then knotted in a loop to form a stop. Hook snoods are attached to the loops

Expanded metal lure. (A) loop or swivel, (B) 28 to 35 lb. line passing through lure and holes in 'Lumina' strip, (C) loop or swivel, (D) hook attached close to lure on 19 to 23 lb. line, (E) 'Lumina' strip

postponing and eventually forgetting it.

I have evolved a variation on the baited spoon theme, in which a strip of expanded metal, such as that used for loud speaker fronts, is utilised.

The expanded metal can be cut into the shape of a flatfish, and on one of these baited lures, measuring $7\frac{1}{4}$ in. × 4 in. I have taken bass, eels, flounders, spur dogfish, etc. Much smaller lures may, of course, be utilised with every success.

It is in my opinion, particularly important to attach to each lure, a strip of 'Lumina', a highly luminous plastic which, incidentally, may also be attached with advantage, to normal hook-baits. These expanded metal lures work much better where there is a current. They do not spin, as do the orthodox baited spoons, which can be constructed by the 'do-it-yourself' angler out of plastic or stainless steel dessert spoons. The stainless steel variety are normally more successful than are those made of plastic, this is probably due to the flash of the bright metal proving more attractive to the fish.

Here is another original idea which may well improve your chances of success. Obtain some tiny plastic or metal salt spoons, cut off the

handles and drill a small hole into one end of the spoon and attach a swivel. Attach the other end of the swivel to the snood or trace, just above your hook which has been baited in an orthodox way. The tiny spoon, particularly if it is bright metal will help to attract the fish to your bait, especially so if the current gives movement to the spoon.

Bait additives

The competitive angler should improve his catches by using additives, such as pilchard oil, either on the bait or in its close proximity. These additives do quite definitely act as fish attractors and they have, in this respect, proved their true worth by helping me to win many competitive events.

In order to introduce, say, pilchard oil into the bait, various novel ideas have been successfully employed, these include hypodermic syringes, fountain pen fillers, oil cans, and other similar devices. A small strip of felt coiled around the line just above the hook, will if soaked in the oil, gradually release a slick for quite a long period.

When competition fishing, I have had great

(above) A catch of bass, flounders, and eels taken on a trace of two baited spoons

(Below) Pilchard-oil sinker. After soaking in pilchard oil for twenty-four hours before fishing, the felt pad releases a fish-attracting oil slick

success, particularly with codling, when using a sinker which I designed. It is hollowed out and has perforated sides. To save the trouble of boring a block of lead, ordinary lead piping can be used. Plug the hollow centre with felt or cotton wool—a substance which will hold a quantity of pilchard oil. The oil will gradually disperse in the region of the baited hooks. I can assure you that this idea really does work, just try it!

When buying pilchard oil always make sure that you are supplied with the 'full-strength' variety in order to gain the greatest advantage from using it.

'Rubby-dubby' cubes containing pilchard oil are obtainable and each packet is accompanied by a number of small mesh nets for holding them. These cubes can be used in place of a casting weight, and in fact I have utilised them in this manner with very successful results when beach fishing for bass.

The 'rubby-dubby'

A 'rubby-dubby' is used mainly when boat angling to create a lane or path of fish morsels, or

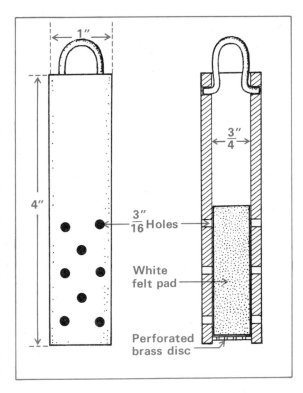

(above) Black bream, a migratory fish of the warmer waters of the south and west

(opposite) An obliging fish, the cod is to be caught from boats in water up to 250 fathoms deep as well as from the shallow beaches around the coast

(right) The mouth of the pollack, large enough to place a man's fist inside, is a good indication of this species' voracious appetite

offal, which slowly disperses downtide and so attracts fish to the anglers' baited hooks. Fine mesh net bags or similar containers are lowered over the side of the boat, and this not only attracts fish but it also holds them in the vicinity of the boat. The filling of fish, offal, crabs, etc., should be beaten to a pulp, or alternatively it can be put through a mincing machine. One very effective variation on this theme can be achieved by attaching a domestic mincer to the side of the boat, in such a manner that any fish or offal passing through it drops straight into the sea. Oily fish, such as mackerel, pilchards, or herrings, make admirable mincing or pulping material.

Modified versions of the rubby-dubby can be used when competitive rock or pier angling, and in this connection the ingenuity of the angler in devising his own variations may well pay dividends. Indeed, a rubby-dubby can be used by a beach angler if he anchors it in position near the spot he intends to fish.

It should be noted that, in addition to the 'lane' created by the rubby-dubby, the addition of blood and/or oil additives, either on, or in the vicinity of the baited hook, proves particularly attractive to dogfish and in fact to all members of the shark family, which includes tope.

When boat fishing, the depth to which the rubby-dubby is lowered depends largely upon the species being fished. For instance, when shark fishing, the bag may be only partly submerged thus allowing the action of the boat to swirl it about. It may also be attached to the anchor rope, either just below the surface, or at any intermediate depth. Sometimes shark and tope will make a grab at the bag, literally tearing it to pieces.

It is always a good plan to try the rubby-dubby at varying depths, but of course if you are seeking essentially bottom-feeding fish, then the logical position for the rubby-dubby bag is, of course, right on the sea-bed.

The best period of the tide

It is surprising to note that many anglers seem to be under the quite mistaken impression that fishing is productive only on the incoming tide and therefore they finish as soon as the ebb commences. When fishing in areas unfamiliar to me, I have often noted this, what is to me, strange attitude. Local anglers have invariably told me that 'Nobody troubles to fish the ebb,

you will only catch fish as the tide comes in', or words to that effect. Despite this 'advice', and taking into account my general experience, I have continued to fish the ebb right down to low water and have found that the best fishing sometimes actually occurred during this period. This is a point well worth noting; the periods covering an hour or so before high water to an hour or so after as well as the corresponding period either side of low water can be most productive.

It is, of course, impossible to generalise, for much depends upon local conditions, but the above are my findings when related to the most favourable fishing periods of the tide.

Daylight or darkness?

In competitive angling, undoubtedly the heaviest catches of fish are taken during the hours of daylight, for the very simple reason that most competitive events actually take place during the day rather than at night. There are, however, many species, for instance tope, conger, codling, silver eels, and dogfish, which feed more avidly during the hours of darkness. Tope, which invariably take a bait more freely at night, present quite a problem to the beach angler during the hours of darkness because he frequently has no idea whether a hooked tope is a hundred yards away, or whether it has run inwards and is virtually under his feet. To a somewhat lesser degree the boat angler is in a similar position, so that one may with quite a degree of truth, say that night fishing in the sea is not so straightforward as it is in daylight.

Often there are conditions which encourage fish to come much closer inshore at night. Typically, bass will sometimes go completely off feed during daylight hours when there is a period of really hot, calm weather, and in consequence the angler at such times often gives up in desperation. He should try night fishing when the same bass could well give him quite an agreeable surprise. I have had this experience on many occasions. And while there can be no hard and fast rule concerning the merits of fishing at night rather than by day, for much depends not only upon prevailing conditions but also upon the species of fish sought, the logical aspect is that the fish simply have to feed sometime and the angler's chances of success must, inevitably, depend upon his being in the correct place at that precise time. A fact which may not coincide

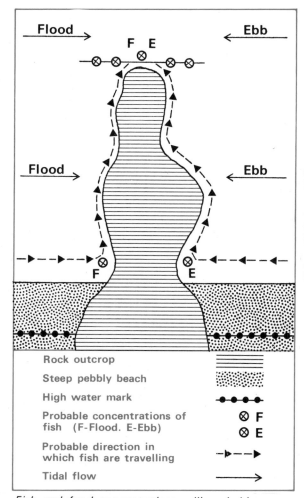

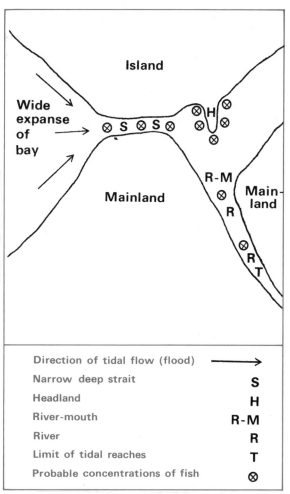

Rock outcrop	≡≡≡≡
Steep pebbly beach	⠐⠂⠒
High water mark	•─•─•─•
Probable concentrations of fish (F-Flood. E-Ebb)	⊗ F ⊗ E
Probable direction in which fish are travelling	–▸– –▸
Tidal flow	──────▸

Direction of tidal flow (flood)	──────▸
Narrow deep strait	**S**
Headland	**H**
River-mouth	**R-M**
River	**R**
Limit of tidal reaches	**T**
Probable concentrations of fish	⊗

Fish and food concentrations will probably occur: (left) to the left of the outcrop when wind is with tide and right of the outcrop on an ebb tide when wind is against tide; (right) where water converges

with the timing of a competition.

Fishing a moving bait

The effectiveness of imparting some occasional movement to the bait cannot be too strongly emphasised. Rather than allowing your bait to lie in the same position throughout the whole of one cast, reel in a yard or so, pause, and then repeat the process. This occasional movement will often make an appreciable difference to your catches. I have watched the actions of flatfish in relation to both a stationary and a moving bait. While the fish will often regard a stationary bait with some indifference, the effect of moving it only for a few inches is to stir them into sudden

in fast tide run through narrow straight, where head-land forms natural barrier to unimpeded progress of fish, in and around a river to the limit of its tidal reaches

action. Quite frequently as a result of this movement they make a sudden dive for the bait, perhaps under the impression that if they do not, they will lose the chance of catching it.

It will of course, be appreciated that this periodical bait movement is only practicable on beaches free of weed, rocks, stones, and other underwater obstacles.

Casting

Quite one of the most controversial subjects in angling is casting. Let us therefore examine casting techniques and their effect upon competitive angling.

Long casting from piers, rocks, and beaches,

A splendid trio of tope from the Menai Straits in Wales

undoubtedly has its merits, and conversely, it may quite rightly be said also to have its demerits. Firstly, one must face the fact that some anglers are so proud of their casting prowess that in order to impress, they often cast such unnecessarily long distances, that their terminal tackle enters the water at a point well beyond where the fish happen to be feeding at that particular time.

Under such circumstances it becomes evident that these casting fanatics fail utterly and completely to satisfy the primary object of their angling, which is of course, to catch fish. On the other hand, there are conditions where the ability to cast a great distance proves to be a vital asset. Undoubtedly, these are occasions when the fish are feeding some distance out and it is under these circumstances that the long-distance caster really comes into his own. For this reason alone it may be said that he possesses a fishing ability over those of his fellow competitors who are less competent at casting.

The conditions under which exceptionally long-distance casting is essential to success, are however, very few and far between. For this reason, providing Mr. Average Caster is one who applies an intelligent knowledge to his technique he will invariably hold his own at most events.

Here are some points concerning the ability to long cast and its relation to competitive angling:

Merits

1. It enables the competitor to reach out to fish feeding at a distance from the shore, pier, or rocks.

2. In crowded events, it enables the competitor to place his baited terminal tackle beyond the barrier of constantly descending sinkers cast by less proficient contestants.

3. If the tide is flowing towards the pier, etc., fish swimming with the tide will reach the long-caster's bait before that of other competitors.

4. Long casting can assist the angler to clear rocks and heavy weed beds, etc.

Demerits

1. The long-distance caster can sometimes prove to be a positive menace in crowded beach or pier events, particularly so if his terminal tackle lands beyond that of other competitors and

is carried by currents across their lines and tackle. This can happen no matter what type of sinker is used.

2. When fishing a pier event and the tide is flowing away from the ranks of competitors, those baits lying nearest to the pier will be the first to be seen by fish travelling downtide. Those who have cast the furthest will then be at a disadvantage.

3. In some areas, masses of floating weed drift across and foul the lines and eventually carry the baited tackle right inshore. Normally under such conditions, the further one casts the more weed one is likely to gather on the line, sometimes to the extent of making fishing virtually impossible. This is very noticeable where strong tidal currents run parallel to the beach. This is not mere hearsay, but has been a personal experience on more than one occasion.

4. Modern reel lines are invariably nylon monofilament, a substance which has a high degree of stretch. Glass fibre rods are very resilient and the combined effects of both tend to absorb a firm strike made against a taking fish, particularly when the fish happens to be some distance away from the rod tip. In this respect, the long-distance caster has less chance of driving the hook in with force. Various practical experiments in this connection have proved to me that lines of braided terylene, used in conjunction with a stiff action, built cane rod, take far more bass than tubular glass rods of similar length, used in conjunction with nylon monofilament, which incidentally, has four times the elasticity of terylene.

So, there are arguments for and against long-distance casting.

Striking the fish

When should the angler strike at a biting fish? It is quite impossible to generalise, as some anglers are inclined to do, and much depends upon the technique employed by the individual. However, of this you may be sure, very few anglers will agree which is the most effective method of striking. Bearing this in mind, it may perhaps be expedient for me to discuss the broad principles involved.

Bass, for example, will sometimes hook themselves, as indeed will many other species, but the bass is very quick both on the mark and off it. There is no doubt that it is the angler who holds his rod and is ready for instant striking, who will invariably prove to be the most consistently successful bass fisher. A bass bite may register as merely a light 'tap, tap', in which case you should strike immediately, for although this may be followed by a second, more pronounced bite, it is my experience that bass will seldom return for a second bite at the same bait. On another occasion, the bass may pick up the bait and run in towards you. Under such circumstances a rapid recovery of line is imperative and whilst so doing it is advisable to keep striking, for by so doing, it is feasible that you will drive the hook home.

However, many bass are lost when the line suddenly becomes slack, so remember, at all times keep the rod tip up and the line as tight as possible. If the bass runs away from you stripping line from the reel, you should strike as soon as possible, despite the fact that it is quite likely that the fish will, in this instance, hook itself. If you are in any doubt whether or not a bass has taken, assume that it has and strike, and keep on striking, for by employing this technique you are certainly not losing anything, and may perhaps be gaining the capture of a fair-sized fish.

There are those who regard the striking of a biting flatfish as being entirely unnecessary, assuming that the flatfish will normally eventually swallow both hook and bait. Plaice and flounders particularly, will do just that. However, dabs appear to be rather adept at sucking the bait from the hook, and for this reason it is advisable to strike at the initial bite. It should be remembered that the mouths of most species of flatfish are relatively small and in consequence, appropriately small hooks and baits should be used. The argument against allowing a flatfish time to actually swallow the baited hook, is of course, that such action results in the fish, irrespective of its size, becoming so injured that it cannot possibly survive the withdrawal of the hook and subsequent return to the water.

It is also said by some that codling will hook themselves. This is not my experience, and there have been numerous occasions when if I had not been holding my rod and ready to strike I would certainly have lost, rather than won, a competitive event. I maintain therefore, that the angler who holds his rod and is ready to strike at the rather sharp bite which is associated with these fish, will most certainly score over those who are content to leave their rods propped up against a pier railing, or against the gunwhale of a boat. These remarks apply, albeit to some lesser extent, to whiting.

Congers sometimes give a preliminary light knock, almost as though they are toying with the bait, as indeed they frequently are. When they show indications of moving away with the bait, it is the time to strike. These fish will often hook themselves by swallowing the baited hook.

Skate and rays despite the size to which the fish grow, will sometimes give quite a gentle bite, and the angler should not be too eager to strike. Instead, wait until they are moving away steadily and then strike hard. Like conger and some species of flatfish, skate and rays often swallow the baited hook.

The manner in which tope take, can be quite unpredictable. It may, for instance, register no more than a small movement on the rod tip, and then, moving slowly at first but at an ever increasing rate, the fish will strip line. Do not strike on the initial take but allow the fish to run for 50 or 60 yards or more and then strike very hard. Conversely, a tope bite may be indicated by the line falling completely slack, in which case the fish is probably running towards you; recover line as rapidly as possible, striking whilst you are retrieving. If a tope hooks itself, you may see the unattended rod speeding out to sea, or disappearing overboard. Indeed, this may happen on the tope's initial run, irrespective of whether it has been hooked or not, so never leave your rod unattended unless the reel check is on and the star drag is set at a minimum.

Mullet have small, soft mouths, and in consequence, the striking of these relatively timid fish should be a rapid, but very gentle action. When a mullet has been hooked it should not only be played most carefully but, for safety's sake, be lifted out of the water by a landing net. It is very easy for the hook to tear from its mouth.

Experience will invariably enable the angler to distinguish between the bite of one species and another, and accordingly, to employ the striking technique appropriate to each. Remember, when striking a fish, less effort is needed to set a relatively small fine-wire hook, than those used for conger fishing.

Finally, never use too large a bait on too small a hook, or your efforts at striking a biting fish may prove of no avail. The hook is merely shrouded with protective padding.

A 'floating' sinker

This is a hint which could well save you losing many sinkers and terminal tackle, and it could also prevent the loss of a great number of fish.

When shore fishing over rocks and heavily weeded areas, your terminal tackle will frequently become snagged, and as a result it may be lost. In order to minimise this possibility, dispense with the lead sinker and tie a flat pebble in its place. Choose one about the same weight as your normal sinker and place it inside a piece of nylon stocking, mutton cloth, or stockinette, and secure the bag to the trace by a piece of weak line. If the 'sinker' becomes caught up in either weed, or rock, the weaker line will break, or the pebble will tear from its flimsy container. However, if the weight does not snag, once it is on the move, it will come skimming along on the surface, and thus clear all intervening obstacles.

After all, pebbles cost nothing and there are usually plenty lying about on the beach. Lead sinkers are not only relatively expensive but no matter how flat they may be they will not come to the surface in the manner of a flat pebble. This idea has now become quite a common practice in rocky and heavily weeded areas such as the Menai Straits.

And finally, on the subject of losing leads, never place them on soft wet sand. You will be amazed at the speed at which they disappear!

From a skin-diver's viewpoint

When considering various techniques, the competition sea angler may well profit from the comments made by a skin-diver:

1. Most metal objects, for example brass paternosters, swivels, streel traces, lead sinkers etc., are as a result of their reflective properties, very obvious to the eye in sunlit waters.

2. Monofilament line glints underwater. (This rather contradicts those who claim that line is invisible when underwater.)

3. Seen from underwater, any form of line becomes greatly magnified in diameter.

4. Worm baits, when suspended, do not look as natural as when they are lying on the sea-bed.

5. Paternosters are more conspicuous than a leger trace used without any form of metal attachment.

6. The impact of a lead sinker upon the surface of the water causes audible and visual disturbances, which scatter fish.

7. Some of the largest fish are seen swimming quite close inshore.

8. More fish are normally to be found under piers and alongside pier piles, than on ground a hundred yards or so away. This (as I have repeatedly found) is a strong argument for dropping one's baited hooks directly below the pier, rather than casting a long distance away from it.

9. The undersides of floats are very obvious, when viewed underwater. For this reason, the use of clear, plastic floats (such as bubble-floats) is an advantage. Unfortunately all forms of line descending from the float are very obvious to the eye.

10. Comparatively small fish, when hooked in the region of obstructions or of weeds can give to the angler an entirely mistaken impression of their size, due to their becoming entangled with such obstructions.

11. The fact that skin-divers definitely see more specimen fish in an area than are ever taken by anglers at that place would suggest that these larger fish have, by virtue of their age, become well educated in the matter of baited hooks and that they are, in consequence, very difficult for the angler to catch. Of one thing I am perfectly certain, and that is, these old-timers have an uncanny knack of removing your bait from the hook, without themselves becoming hooked in the process!

Line control when boat angling

While it is not always possible when boat angling, to avoid one line from tangling with another, the possibility of this time and temper wasting occurrence can often be greatly minimised. Those fishing from the bow of the boat should use the heaviest sinkers, the anglers next to them slightly lighter ones, and so on, right down to the stern, where those anglers can fish the lightest weights and let their tackle stream downtide, well away from the others. This is sound practice which, if conscientiously applied, can work effectively in all normal conditions. If a plan for rotation is agreed before angling commences, then everyone has an equal chance.

However, although I am a firm advocate of the principle of fishing as light as possible, one must be sensible. In boat angling contests, particularly those concerned with fish such as tope and skate, it is downright selfish for any competitor to

A fine mixed catch from Achill Head, Ireland

employ lines or tackle which are incapable of handling the fish. An angler can virtually monopolise an appreciable amount of fishing time, thus handicapping those anglers who have sportingly withdrawn their tackle in order not to impede the successful playing of the fish. So please, do restrict the use of light tackle to those occasions where they are not foreseeably likely to curtail the sport of others.

Spare reel spools

Some manufacturers supply as standard, an additional spool with each reel. Others will supply extra spools for an appropriate additional charge.

Undoubtedly it is an advantage to carry a spare spool which can be loaded with a heavier or a lighter line. Apart from other considerations, one can lose a fantastic amount of fishing time whilst doing no more than unravelling a bird's nest.

However in the absence of a spare reel spool, always be sure to include a reel or two of spare line in your tackle box.

It is appropriate in this chapter to include a few useful hints which may well prove to be of some help to the competitive angler.

Although no event would be settled without accurate scales, it is not difficult to imagine a situation where the following formula could be extremely useful. To ascertain the *approximate* weight in pounds of a fish: multiply the square

A helping hand is available to straighten-out the terminal tackle. A sense of comradeship such as this is not unusual in sea angling competitions

of the girth (the measurement to be taken at the thickest point) by the length (from point of mouth to crotch of tail) then divide the result by 800. (All measurements should be taken in inches.) Example: 10 in. girth squared is 100; length 20 in. multiplied by 100 is 2,000; 2,000 divided by 800 goes exactly $2\frac{1}{2}$ times, therefore the approximate weight of the fish would be $2\frac{1}{2}$ lb. On the same basis, a 30 in. fish, with a girth of 20 in. should weigh approximately 15 lb. In actual practice, it is surprising how accurate this formula is.

Make a list of the various items you need for competitive fishing and tick each item off before setting out. How exasperating it is to find that something vital, maybe even the bait, has been forgotten.

Remember to coat your bait with additives, (pilchard oil, etc.) if competition rules permit. They can greatly enhance your chances of success.

Try not to be hide-bound in your approach, if you hear of, or see, a new device designed for improving the angler's chances of success, try it out. Never dismiss it as of no account, it could be the difference between success and failure.

When engaged in competitive fishing, always have a spare trace or paternoster ready for

immediate attachment. Much valuable time can be wasted if you have to search your other gear in order to replace lost terminal tackle. Also have, spare hooks, loose and ready tied, ready for immediate use. It is so easy for the lost seconds and minutes to add up to as much as an hour or so if one is not very careful.

To keep peeler and soft crabs alive for the maximum possible time, obtain one or more plastic food containers and drill a number of small holes in each lid. Place fresh seaweed in each container and keep soft and peeler crabs in separate containers. Dead or mutilated crabs must not be included. Place the containers in the coldest part of your fridge, but not in the freezing compartment itself. Inspect the crabs periodically, removing any dead ones. Renew the existing seaweed with fresh weed at least once a week, and if possible remove the crabs, place them in a sack and take them for a dip in the sea. This will help to prolong the keeping period, which can, believe it or not, extend to several weeks. Never use fresh water to damp the seaweed or the crabs, and never leave dead crabs in the containers.

There is nothing objectionable in keeping crabs in a domestic fridge, always providing that you periodically renew the seaweed, which will otherwise tend to decay. It is also an asset to have, as. I have, a reasonably tolerant wife!

To be prepared for every eventuality, always take two rods and two reels with you, just in case one or the other should let you down; and always check the competition rules to see if spinning is likely to be permitted. If it is, then go prepared.

If it is a beach contest, remember that a rod rest will be an asset. It is not suggested that you should leave your rod in a rest whilst fishing, but it is preferable to lying the rod and reel down on

A difficult mark to fish but an unattended rod still gives the fish the chance to nip the bait and run before the angler can strike

shingle or sand when setting up tackle, and whilst baiting up.

Always wear suitable all-weather clothing. Nothing is more frustrating than to get thoroughly wet, or feel really cold. It can in fact, make all the difference between your winning or losing the event.

If the competition is likely to take place partly or wholly during the hours of darkness make sure that you have lighting.

Useful accessories which the angler should always carry include a sharp knife, a disgorger, a pair of long-nosed pliers, a clean piece of towelling, a piece of carborundum stone for adding that little extra keenness to your hook, a rule or measuring stick for checking whether or not your fish are within the size limits, a reliable spring balance for weighing your fish, and protective gloves if you are likely to be handling heavy fish and wire traces. A small first aid outfit should also be included in your kit.

The presence of seals

It's a fallacy to imagine that because a seal happens to be in the area alloted to you in a competition, your chances of catching fish therefore become negligible. My friends and I have caught bass and other species when a seal has been watching us from a nearby rock within casting distance. The fact that the seal is there actually signifies the presence of fish.

In September 1968, I was fishing a competition at Holyhead Breakwater and just below me was an enormous bull seal which occasionally came out of the water and lay on a weed-covered

An angler leans into a fish during a competition on Tynemouth pier

rock. Despite his presence, I caught three pollack and seven wrasse, totalling 12 lb. 14 oz. and easily won the event. One interesting feature of the day's fishing resulted from a hefty bite, which when played to the surface, proved to be a conger in the 15 to 20 lb. class. When this fish came to the surface, spinning violently as congers sometimes do, I realised that there was no chance of lifting it 30 ft. or so from the surface of the water to the top of the breakwater wall on my 19 lb. breaking strain line. Meanwhile, the old bull seal lay on his rock watching the event, as much as to say, 'You've got some hopes of landing *that* fish'. Eventually, and inevitably, my line snapped close to the hook, and momentarily the conger was on the surface. Quick as a flash, the seal slithered down his rock and into the water, making a bee-line for the fish. Whether he ever got it, I shall never know, as what ensued took place well under the surface, away from the prying eyes of man.

This, however, I do know. Not only are seals fond of conger but the angler can catch fish with seals in the immediate vicinity.

Angling courtesy

When taking part in competitive events, and indeed in any form of angling, be courteous to your fellow anglers and never be guilty of turning angling into wrangling.

Do not, if you can possibly avoid it, try to scrounge bait as this can often give your friends and acquaintances an entirely mistaken impression of you. I have found in my lifetime of angling that bait-scroungers can be notoriously unpopular.

When boat angling, always reel in your tackle when a companion has hooked a large fish. By failing to observe this act of common courtesy, you may not only be the indirect cause of the angler losing his fish, but also be responsible for causing a hopeless tangle of lines, including your own. This courtesy should also apply to shore-based events, when for instance, an angler has hooked a tope or a conger.

During beach, pier, or rock angling events, always endeavour, to the best of your ability, to cast straight and not across the lines of other competitors. Nothing is more exasperating than to fish alongside an angler who fails to observe this courtesy. Apart from all else, the time that is wasted sorting out the 'knitting' can often be the difference between success and failure.

Never, in 'pegged' contests (and this includes fishing from fixed places in boats) encroach upon the space allotted to another competitor. In short, try to act as you would wish others to act towards you.

Before ending this chapter, may I once again stress the utmost importance of presenting your bait or lure to the fish in the most natural and attractive manner possible? You may well be equipped with the finest, most up to date tackle which money can buy, but it will not serve its purpose to the full unless you can successfully tempt the fish. They are just not interested in your tackle as such, but purely and simply in what lies at the end of it, namely the bait or lure. Try to make it irresistible to the fish, and then you may be said to be well on the way to conquering them. This is the technique which I unfailingly adopt, and believe me, it pays.

Finally, two points regarding beach fishing and casting. Always wash your hands free of sand before handling your reel or line, as sand and grit can easily be transmitted to the reel and then into its mechanism which will cause quite needless wear.

Remember that the size of your bait can have a tremendous effect upon casting potential. For instance, the air resistance of baits such as peeler and soft crabs is greater than that of a single ragworm or lugworm. Similarly, while whole mackerel or whole herrings are excellent baits for tope fishing, they become rather unwieldy when cast from the beach. Under conditions where sheer distance is essential in order to reach the fish, endeavour to streamline your bait as much as possible. This can be achieved, for example, by slicing long, thin fillets.

In order to appreciate this point, try casting without bait and note the distance you achieve. Then bait up and try a further cast. You may be surprised at the appreciable reduction in distance if the bait happens to be bulky, for example portions of fish, as compared with the more streamlined baits, such as single lugworms or single ragworms.

(opposite) Adequate weighing facilities are essential at any competition. Final adjustments are made to the balance before accurately recording the fish's weight

Useful Knots

As new materials for fishing lines have become available so new knots have had to be devised to cope with their various peculiarities. This is particularly true of nylon monofilament which has a great tendency to slip no matter which knot is used. Another difficulty with nylon is that any knot, regardless of the efficiency of its design, will weaken it. In choosing a knot, the angler should always bear this point in mind and the knots given here are all eminently suited to their various tasks and result in the minimum loss of line strength.

The way in which a knot is tied can have a tremendous effect upon its efficiency. Always take time over tying any knot and make sure that each turn is snugged down into its correct position when tightened. This can greatly be aided by lubricating the nylon with saliva before finally tightening the knot with an evenly applied pressure.

Braided Terylene is another popular material for fishing lines but presents entirely different knotting problems. Slipping, the bugbear of nylon, is not a drawback of this material. Its main disadvantage is that it tends to cut itself when ordinary knots are used and after some abrasion, often frays and becomes whiskery. A special knot for Terylene lines which has been designed to overcome these difficulties is included. The same care is needed when tying this knot as with nylon if the best results are to be obtained.

Tucked four-turn half blood knot
1. *Pass end of nylon through eye of hook or swivel and take four turns around standing part.*
2. *Pass end through loop next to the eye and pass back through large loop.*
3. *Draw tight and cut off free end.*

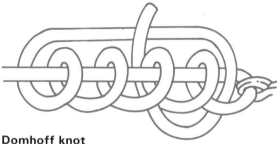

Domhoff knot
1. *Double line along length of hookshank and starting from the eye whip at least eight turns around the shank and loop of line. Pass end of line through loop A after final turn.*
2. *Pull on standing part to tighten knot against the eye.*

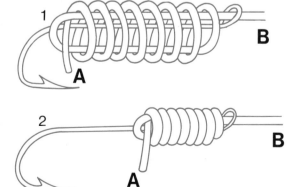

Constructing a loop in braided Terylene
1. *Form loop of required length and using a stop for the wrapping whip end A around standing part. After whipping up the standing part for at least $1\frac{1}{2}$ in., end A should be whipped down again over the first set of whipping.*
2. *Make an overhand knot on one side of the loop whilst holding the coils tightly.*
3. *Make an overhand knot on the other side of the loop.*
4. *Finally an overhand knot is tied in end A to stop it from slipping undone before cutting off near knot.*

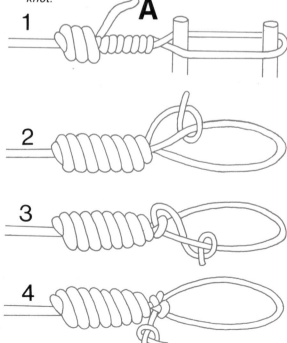

Blood bight knot

1. Bend end of nylon back on itself to form loop A.
2. Twist loop A around line as shown to form loop B.
3. Pass loop A through loop B.
4. Tighten knot and cut off free end.

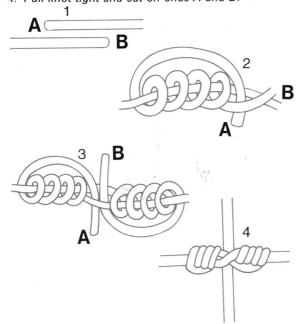

Double overhand loop knot

1. Bend end of line back on itself to form loop A.
2. Take two turns around standing part of doubled line with loop A.
3. Pull loop A tight and cut off free end.

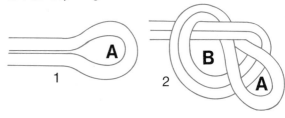

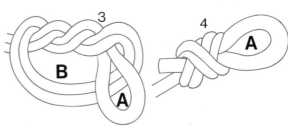

Double four-fold blood knot

1. Place the two ends to be joined alongside each other.
2. Take four turns around the standing part of B with end A and turn back and pass through gap where end B crosses standing part of A.
3. Take four turns around the standing part of A with end B and turn back and pass through gap next to end A but from the opposite side.
4. Pull knot tight and cut off ends A and B.

Making a monofilament paternoster

1. Form a blood loop as illustrated. Place pencil in loop A and pull knot tight.
2. A normal hook length can then be attached by passing the loop of the hook length over the blood loop, passing the other end with the hook attached through the blood loop and then pulling tight.

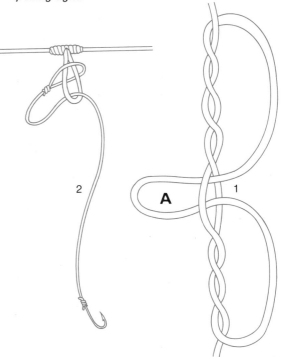